SATAN
GOD
OR
SCHIZOAFFECTIVE
DISORDER 295.7

The life and times of
TEXAS GUITAR LEGEND NATHON DEES

This is the true story of one man's amazing struggle with reality, religion and mental illness. As you read you will join in with Texas Guitar Legend Nathon Dees as he takes you on an adventure of his life and how he finally broke free from a Christian society and learned to cope with de habilitating mental illness in a unique and interesting way.

SATAN, GOD OR SCHIZOAFFECTIVE DISORDER 295.7 THE LIFE AND TIMES OF TEXAS GUITAR LEGEND NATHON DEES

INTRODUCTION

My name was once the Rev. Nathon Q. Dees, former Associate Pastor of the First Baptist Church of Sheldon, in my home town of Sheldon, Texas, an alumni of The Abundant Life School of Ministry, a prospective member of the Alliance Christian motorcycle ministry and a Free Mason. I was a self employed veteran and held a license for home building, construction, remodeling, renovations, waste water systems and owned a custom motorcycle shop.

Now my I'm just plain old Nathon living from day to day on a beach in Jaco, Costa Rica on a US government pension check for being mentally disabled as the result of Schizoaffective Disorder 295.7 as defined by the DSM IV.

I delivered myself from Satanic possession, Demonic oppression, angels, devils, heaven, hell and the church but it cost me everything including my wife, friends and even my country to know and accept the fact that I was mentally ill and that everything that I believed was a delusion caused by my illness and perpetuated by the lies of Christianity.

Now that I've traded theology books and bibles for psychology and philosophy books it is very clear to me that I was mentally ill even as a small child and the events of my youth that led to my salvation were textbook undiagnosed mental illness. I spent fifteen years of my life institutionalized in the church before I realized that I was sick and needed help, not ancient fairy tells that allowed me to live within a completely delusional world created by the myths of Christian doctrine and folklore.

Schizoaffective disorder 295.7
Definition
Schizoaffective Disorder is basically a cross between a disturbance in thought and a disturbance in mood. Both symptom clusters (depressive/manic and schizophrenic) must exist at the same time (co morbid) to justify a diagnosis of this disorder.
Diagnostic criteria
A. An uninterrupted period of illness during which, at some time, there is either:

☐ (1) a Major Depressive Episode,

☐ (2) a Manic Episode, or

☐ (3) a Mixed Episode

Concurrent with symptoms that meet (4) Criterion A for Schizophrenia.
Note: The Major Depressive Episode must include depressed mood.
(1) Criteria for Major Depressive Episode Five (or more) of the following symptoms have been present during the same 2-week period and represent a change from previous functioning; at least one of the symptoms is either (1) depressed mood or (2) loss of interest or pleasure. **Note:** Do not include symptoms that are clearly due to a general medical condition, or mood-incongruent delusions or hallucinations.

☐ depressed mood most of the day, nearly every day, as indicated by either subjective report (e.g., feels sad or empty) or observation made by others (e.g., appears tearful). Note: In children and adolescents, can be irritable mood.

☐ markedly diminished interest or pleasure in all, or almost all, activities most of the day, nearly every day (as indicated by either subjective account or observation made by others)

☐ Significant weight loss when not dieting or weight gain (e.g., a change of more than 5% of body weight in a month), or decrease or increase in appetite nearly every day. Note: In children, consider failure to make expected weight gains.

☐ Insomnia or hypersomnia nearly every day

☐ Psychomotor agitation or retardation nearly every day (observable by others, not merely subjective feelings of restlessness or being slowed down)

☐ Fatigue or loss of energy nearly every day

☐ Feelings of worthlessness or excessive or inappropriate guilt (which may be delusional) nearly every day (not merely self-reproach or guilt about being sick)

☐ diminished ability to think or concentrate, or indecisiveness, nearly every day (either by subjective account or as observed by others)

☐ Recurrent thoughts of death (not just fear of dying), recurrent suicidal ideation without a specific plan, or a suicide attempt or a specific plan for committing suicide

The symptoms do not meet criteria for a Mixed Episode
The symptoms cause clinically significant distress or impairment in social, occupational, or other important areas of functioning.
The symptoms are not due to the direct physiological effects of a substance (e.g., a drug of abuse, a medication) or a general medical condition (e.g., hypothyroidism).

The symptoms are not better accounted for by Bereavement, i.e., after the loss of a loved one, the symptoms persist for longer than 2 months or are characterized by marked functional impairment, morbid preoccupation with worthlessness, suicidal ideation, psychotic symptoms, or psychomotor retardation.

(2) Criteria for Manic Episode A distinct period of abnormally and persistently elevated, expansive, or irritable mood, lasting at least 1 week (or any duration if hospitalization is necessary).

During the period of mood disturbance, three (or more) of the following symptoms have persisted (four if the mood is only irritable) and have been present to a significant degree:

☐ inflated self-esteem or grandiosity

☐ decreased need for sleep (e.g., feels rested after only 3 hours of sleep)

☐ More talkative than usual or pressure to keep talking

☐ Insomnia or hypersomnia nearly every day

☐ Psychomotor agitation or retardation nearly every day (observable by others, not merely subjective feelings of restlessness or being slowed down)

☐ Flight of ideas or subjective experience that thoughts are racing

☐ Distractibility (i.e., attention too easily drawn to unimportant or irrelevant external stimuli)

☐ Increase in goal-directed activity (either socially, at work or school, or sexually) or psychomotor agitation

☐ Excessive involvement in pleasurable activities that have a high potential for painful consequences (e.g., engaging in unrestrained buying sprees, sexual indiscretions, or foolish business investments)

The symptoms do not meet criteria for a Mixed Episode

The mood disturbance is sufficiently severe to cause marked impairment in occupational functioning or in usual social activities or relationships with others, or to necessitate hospitalization to prevent harm to self or others, or there are psychotic features.

The symptoms are not due to the direct physiological effects of a substance (e.g., a drug of abuse, a medication, or other treatment) or a general medical condition (e.g., hyperthyroidism).

(3) Criteria for Mixed Episode The criteria are met both for a Manic Episode and for a Major Depressive Episode (except for duration) nearly every day during at least a 1-week period.

The mood disturbance is sufficiently severe to cause marked impairment in occupational functioning or in usual social activities or relationships with others, or to necessitate hospitalization to prevent harm to self or others, or there are psychotic features.

The symptoms are not due to the direct physiological effects of a substance (e.g., a drug of abuse, a medication, or other treatment) or a general medical condition (e.g., hyperthyroidism).

(4) Criterion A for Schizophrenia Two (or more) of the following, each present for a significant portion of time during a 1-month period (or less if successfully treated):

☐ Delusions

☐ Hallucinations

☐ disorganized speech (e.g., frequent derailment or incoherence)

☐ Grossly disorganized or catatonic behavior

☐ Negative symptoms, i.e., affective flattening, alogia, or avolition

Only one symptom is required if delusions are bizarre or hallucinations consist of a voice keeping up a running commentary on the person's behavior or thoughts, or two or more voices conversing with each other.
B. During the same period of illness, there have been delusions or hallucinations for at least 2 weeks in the absence of prominent mood symptoms.

C. Symptoms that meet criteria for a mood episode are present for a substantial portion of the total duration of the active and residual periods of the illness.

D. The disturbance is not due to the direct physiological effects of a substance (e.g., a drug of abuse, a medication) or a general medical condition.

Specify if:

☐ **Bipolar Type:** if the disturbance includes a Manic or a Mixed Episode (or a Manic or a Mixed Episode and Major Depressive Episodes)

☐ **Depressive Type:** if the disturbance only includes Major Depressive Episode

Associated features

☐ Learning Problem

☐ Hypoactivity

☐ Psychotic

☐ Euphoric Mood

☐ Depressed Mood

☐ Somatic/Sexual Dysfunction

☐ Hyperactivity

☐ Guilt/Obsession

☐ Odd/Eccentric/Suspicious Personality

☐ Anxious/Fearful/Dependent Personality

☐ Dramatic/Erratic/Antisocial Personality

CHAPTER ONE
IN THE BEGINNING THERE WAS SCHIZOPHRENIA

I was born on June the second 1967 the fifth pregnancy of an RH incompatible couple.

RH incompatibility has links to Schizophrenia. This is a condition where the mother's blood attacks the father's blood within the fetus, it doesn't affect the first child but it gets progressively worse each additional birth. Medicine had overcome this condition completely by the early seventies in the US.

My mom Jody who suffered from severe depression her whole life and my dad Byron who had young adult schizophrenia with hallucinations by his early twenties. I gathered this by the stories he would tell me of seeing and talking to his spirit self when he worked on the dredge boat at night. I attributed the story to the fact that he was a messenger that turned away from God.

He was no less than a genius but had a really twisted perspective of life and the most grandiose self image of anyone you'd ever meet, not just self confident but more God like passing judgment on the world for being less than he was. My father was a very successful self employed business owner with one of the largest electric motor repair and machine shops in Texas, as well as motels, apartments, A/C and electrical companies, rental properties, ice cream parlors, home building and construction companies you name he did it at least once. He was a veteran, a former sheriff's deputy, a Free Mason and a Rotarian.

His mental illness gave him incredible abilities and vision but also added an equal amount of problems but like many who never see a doctor or have a breakdown he used denial therapy. His power of persuasion is so strong that you could be standing there with him and see something happen and he'd ask you if you were sure it really happened in a way that would make you doubt yourself.

My mom Jody had been abused psychologically as a child by her father who was a Christian, which gave her a disliking of religion and hatred towards most men especially my father. She was a good and faithful wife and mother who longed for the day when she could be left alone by everybody and finally just sit and read books which she loved to do. Mom hated Christmas which I agree with. She was and still is the most non bullshit person that I have ever met.

Mom understood that we all had problems and told us to deal with it. I'll never forget the day she told me that she always believed that I would be the child that killed myself. My mom warned me to keep my guard up against suicidal thoughts.

My mom had five pregnancies, first my brother Robert who was a little wild as a teen but after that got married and led a productive and normal life. Robert was a Free Mason and a self taught engineer. My brother Robert was a brilliant and honorable man, He died of cancer at the age of forty nine. He is survived by his wife Patty and his two children Carrie and Chase.

Next, my sister Sherrill who was kind, beautiful and smart, she excelled in school and has made a lifelong career out of learning and going to college. Sherrill was born RH incompatible and had three blood transfusions at birth to stabilize the condition.

Sherrill has Bi Polar 1 disorder and has spent thousands of dollars on doctors and psychiatrist that did more harm than good. She rebounds back and forth from religion to holistic medicine, she is brilliant and a visionary but her life is an emotional roller coaster. One of the reasons that Sherrill was never hospitalized is because her husband Danny is a good man that has always supported her and put up with the illness. They have three children, Twins Lauren and Danny Jr. and a younger daughter named Madison. Byron and Jodie's third child was Damon, who was very special, He had problems like, lazy eye, dyslexia and ADD he was off the scale from the start. He was a hyper active Tasmanian Devil who had been kicked out of school for good by fourteen years old and asked never to come back after bringing a fire arm to school. Damon has been a complete drug addict and alcoholic since thirteen and has been through the best rehabilitation programs in the US. Damon was a thief and a compulsive liar, he has been in prison fifteen of the last twenty years and is currently living in a hospital for drug treatment.

The last we heard he was in a rehab center in Florida and back on his meds. Having Damon as a part of my life has been an absolute and complete terror every since I can remember. For instance; how many times have you had to hold your own drug crazed brother off at gun point or turn him into the police to protect your family? The next pregnancy, the fourth was a late term miss carriage resulting from the increasing RH incompatibility factor in my mom's blood.

Next was me, Nathon the fifth and final child, in fact my mom not only got her tubes tied but she basically stopped having sex. By this time the doctors knew a lot more about RH incompatibility and with my mother's medical history they where prepared for the worst. I was born three weeks pre mature and dying from my own blood. My father took me from the hospital and drove me to The Texas Children's Hospital's special care unit himself with my aunt Mary holding my blue dying body in her arms. At Texas Children's I received thirteen complete blood transfusions before my condition stabilized, every time the RH factor would reach eighteen they would start the process over. On the final attempt my RH level reached twenty one and subsided. My father was told by the doctors that there was a great possibility that I would be mentally ill, either mentally retarded or brilliant but with some problems, I guess I've been both.

CHAPTER TWO
WHAT DID YOU REALLY EXPECT?

Bad blood and poor genetics. It's a good thing we marry for love and looks.
I was already a candidate from genetic inheritance to receive Depressive Bi Polar 2 Disorder from my mom and Young Adult Schizophrenia from my dad.
Not to mention a long history of doctors, priest, pedophiles, murderers and womanizers on both sides of the family. Thanks mom and dad! Now that they had children together I also had a blood disorder that causes retard fetal brain development forming an enlarged neuro vascular system.
I was messed up from the beginning but I guess things could have been much worse.
You know that's the thing with Schizophrenia, ten fingers, ten toes, perfectly normal on the outside and usually extremely intelligent. Who is trying to diagnose a problem with a perfectly healthy child that's bright and happy and has a great imagination?
Even now as an adult I find that since I'm articulate and can communicate with some degree of intelligence people find it hard to believe that I am mentally ill. I have Schizoaffective Disorder 295.7 tattooed on my fore arm and people still don't believe me. I guess mentally ill people are supposed to be stupid, retarded or John Nash before people can accept or understand it. Furthermore it is impossible for a charismatic Christian to accept my illness because it challenges their faith. In retrospect, I feel that I could have been committed to an institution on believing in Christian doctrine alone. The DSM-IV has a section on religious related mental illness that address these issues and rename schizo related symptoms that occur in religion so as not to condemn the religious community to mental illness. I call a duck a duck and schizophrenia is schizophrenia whether in a cultural religious context or not.
I am thankful that there are dedicated healthcare professionals that know and understand what true mental illness is.

CHAPTER THREE
EARLY CHILD HOOD SURVIVAL GUIDE

I had a good family and a happy childhood, my parents didn't even smoke or drink. We had the makings of a normal family but we were a really strange. We just never really did things like the other kid's families did and everyone seemed to talk bad about each other when the other folks weren't around. My parents weren't abusive or anything and the only real terror in our life was Damon whom I'm still convinced was spawned by Satan.

I remember watching children's programming on PBS and thinking that I was supposed to be on those TV shows, I knew someone was searching for me at that very moment, that I was somehow special. I had talent, I could sing and dance and I was smart. in fact; " too smart for my own good" is what I remember them saying about me. When Mr. Rogers would come on TV and encourage us to go to the world of make believe I was already there. I took many trips on Charley the trolley. My imagination was so powerful that everything was real to me. I was afraid of Spider man and Oscar the grouch, and I taught myself to spell watching children's programming on PBS. I would spend hours laying in my front yard looking for four leaf clovers knowing that if anyone could find the way to Brigadoon it was me or laying in the yard with mirrors and my dad's Chariots of the God's book trying to contact aliens so they could find me.

I also remember clearly being captivated by fear at times, having nightmares and both audio and visual hallucinations of ghost and devils as well as what spiritualist refer to as out of body experiences at the age of five. There was a scary television series that came on at night that my parents watched called The Night Gallery. I would sneak down the stairs and watch it from around the corner with Damon. After being exposed to fear and darkness they fueled my nightmares and became my enemy. I always thought something was out to get me and the fear could come on at any time like a chilling wind forecasting doom. I bought my dad a cool looking skull bank for his birthday when I was a kid. I had nightmares of it chasing me down the hall and after that I hid it nearly every day because I was terrified of it.

I had nightmares about my ventriloquist dummy coming to life and killing me so I locked it in the closet at night. I slept with an arsenal of stuffed animals to protect me at night while I hid under the sheets until I was nearly thirteen years old. Even a simple walk through the woods could end in terror if I let my imagination take over. Remember the Creamoltion cough syrup for children add on TV where the spooky trees chased the kids through the forest? That commercial messed me up big time. It seemed like whatever data was input would be the subject matter of my delusions either positive or negative.

By this age I had also suffered two brain Concussions and been hospitalized on numerous occasions. The first, a head injury from a fall. I was playing with Damon and he dared me to climb up high on a platform at my dad's construction sight where he was playing, It's never the fall that hurts it's the landing. The second head injury was from getting run over by a motorcycle that my brother Damon was riding. He was racing my brother Robert and his friend Bobby Carter while I was standing on the roadside watching and cheering them on. As the racers past on their mini bikes Damon lost control and wiped me out, Bobby gave me mouth to mouth and revived me then I retained consciousness in the hospital hours later screaming in terror.

The very day that I was released from the hospital after the motorcycle accident my parents took us to the best restaurant in our town called Western Travelers where we had fried shrimp. I always loved the Western Travelers because they had a water wheel and a stream inside the restaurant with stuffed raccoons playing in the water. That was cool. After the meal my folks were standing in the parking lot talking to friends, When Damon challenged me and our friend Buddy to a race. I was running across the parking lot with my brother Damon when we fell into a freshly poured parking lot slab of terrazzo concrete that got in my eyes and blinded me. Back to Texas Children's again were they removed my eyes from my head to flush out the crushed glass and cement from my eye sockets. If it had taken my dad any longer to get me to the hospital, a rout he knew well by now, I would have been permanently blind. I was blind for approximately six months while the new eye tissue grew into place. Damon had a field day with this, leading me into walls, moving furniture around and hiding things from me. I do remember that my Aunt Emma Lu gave me a toy gun with a light in it and I would run the batteries down just holding it next to the bandages where I could see its dim red light. It was the only comfort in my darkness and Damon would hide it from me on a daily basis just to be cruel. After my eyes got better and I could see again, I was in my father's electric motor repair shop playing barefoot one night when Damon shut off the lights and ran off leaving me in there alone," on purpose ". Well I ran for the door in terror and stepped on a broken bottle that had fallen during my attempted escape and was now on my way back to the hospital getting my foot sewn back together. Eighteen stitches in my foot and I still have the scar today.

It was a very difficult first five years of child hood with many trips to the hospital. One day Damon and my cousins even made a bomb out of gasoline, clay and a wick. I was running across the yard trying to get away from him when he threw it and set me on fire. Hey the bomb really worked.

Fortunately I had been playing in the woods and I had on me fathers leather hunting vest. It saved my life. I only received first and second degree burns on my arms and legs. Damon got in trouble for playing with gasoline and fire and I got in trouble for wearing my dad's new hunting vest without permission and getting it messed up, go figure that. We had a pet alligator named Allie that Damon had caught. Allie lived in our bath tub until mom told us we couldn't keep it. One day when I came home from school Damon had crucified the baby alligator with sixteen penny nails on a tree in the back yard to watch it die. I was pretty devastated by the ordeal.

CHAPTER FOUR
JESUS AND THE FIRE TRUCK

My parents never went to church. My mother had been forced to go by her dad and my dad had many colorful things to say about the church and preachers, and claimed to have a special deal with God. They still both professed to believe in Christianity and God just like most people in the US that don't want to be persecuted or pestered for non belief. After all this was Texas, Jesus the KKK and pecan pie. Who wouldn't believe that?

The only real live parade I had ever seen on my street was for the vacation bible school at the First Baptist Church of Sheldon and man I wanted to be a part of that. They had clowns and rode on fire trucks, threw candy and knew Jesus personally, who wouldn't want to be a part of that. I would go to church with my next door neighbors the Tollar family. They were Yankees from Wisconsin and Mrs. Tollar played the organ in the church. I remember when I was attending Sunday school, the concepts and subject matter of Christian doctrine where so surreal to me. Jesus on the cross, Jonah in a whale, Daniel with the lions, people hearing voices and seeing visions and most of all, The Devil and his demons.

Even at this young age I was experiencing grandiose delusions of spiritual callings and divine purpose and believed that Satan was trying to kill me because I was chosen by God for a special purpose and that my brother Damon was possessed by the Devil.

I have found time and time again in the church that if you possess any kind of special talent , ability or charisma Christians think that God has created you for his will and purpose and they promote delusions of grandeur to anyone with abilities out of the ordinary especially if they can use you to their advantage.

CHAPTER FIVE
INTRODUCTION TO PLANET SCHOOL

At five years old I entered into public school and came into contact with people outside of my family or church for the first time. It was a fascinating new world to me and I began to excel. After only a short while in school I was given a mental aptitude test and scored with the intelligence of an average ten year old at age five. I needed to be taught the basics like any other child but my ability to think and reason or just plain figure things out on my own was far superior to other children. After the testing was completed I was selected to be a charter student in the first magnet school program in Houston for gifted and talented students. My father who has a great many issues of his own thought that this was some kind of conspiracy and told the school " You're not bussing my kid to some Nigger school in Houston! " it's possible that he thought that this was a program for inter racial busing and did not understand what the program was about. Or maybe he thought it was a special ed program like they had requested for Damon and he was sheltering us and didn't want to admit that his kids were different or had anything wrong with them. He still won't today. Regardless I didn't get to go and I missed the greatest opportunity of my educational life. I think that had I went into the program that not only would caring professionals have nurtured my many talents and abilities but that someone would have diagnosed my illness in it's early stages and I would not be mentally disabled today nor would I have been sucked into religion or drugs, but you never can tell can you. The teachers told my parents that they could not provide the kind of attention that I needed and that they were afraid that I would get bored if I stayed in public school and shut down. They were right, by the third grade I had stopped doing class work or participating in class, I passed everything by having high test scores.

I wasn't a discipline problem until the fifth Grade but I saw school as illogical. All that I saw were a bunch of glorified housewives reciting information out of text books that already had answers in them and that any trained monkey could do the same and that school was a waist of my time and that I had a greater purpose to fulfill than being a cog in the wheel of society.

I really believed that I belonged in a think tank somewhere being raised by scientist and solving problems and writing text books for teachers, not on the other end of the food chain. All it took was one unmotivated old hag named Mrs. Maxwell in the fourth grade to make me stop participating in class all together.

To educators like Mrs. Maxwell: "If you don't like teaching or children you should get another job instead of ruining the educational experience for others."

The power struggles began and I loved the attention. It was really as if my child development was on high speed and that I was experiencing adolescent rebellion in my grade school years. In fact I could easily say that I have been about ten years ahead of my peers in every phase of life. For instance I had already conquered eight years of drugs and alcohol as well as ended a very emotional four year sexual relationship and was a veteran performing artist with many trade skills at the time that most kids were smoking their first joint or just graduating high school. It blew me away when I would see someone make it all the way to college clean and then blow it on Drugs or alcohol as soon as they were on their own for the first time.

I had started experimenting with drugs in Junior high partied through high school " well the ninth grade twice" got a GED and was clean and sober by time for college. What dumb asses. What a waist.

In the sixth grade I failed my first class, it was English of all things and it was my favorite teacher Mrs. Miller. Hell I didn't care, my parents were pre occupied with Damon who had already been thrown out of school by this time and was constantly getting in trouble with the law. It didn't seem to matter whether I did school work or not. I just stopped bringing home report cards and after a while they stopped asking for them. I met my girlfriend when she was in the sixth grade so I failed a year of school on purpose just so I could stay with her another year before we went to high school. I failed another year and they moved me up anyway because I was such a disruption to the other students.

I went to the nurse and counselors office regularly during Jr. High and I explained to them in great detail what was going on in my mind and that I had been having thoughts of suicide and issues, but I was never referred to a doctor or psychiatrist and in fact I was told that I had an attitude problem. I even wrote a story about what I was going through and the difficulties of being a teenager that won fourth place in The Houston Post state wide writing composition contest. Everybody read the story and no one really understood what I was trying to say. I was never entered into a special education program for mental illness because in Texas everything is based on exams and test scores and not only could I pass any exam I had an IQ of one hundred forty at thirteen and I had not participated in class since the third grade. School was a joke.

CHAPTER SIX
SEX, DRUGS AND ROCK-N-ROLL

By the sixth grade I was experimenting with different personalities and trying to establish what I was going to be. I was in band because I loved music and I wanted to be a musician so it seemed necessary to learn music. But not being a jock and not fitting in with the band geeks I had to establish myself socially. Being a red neck was too easy in Texas so I established Rock-n-Roll music as the voice of my personality and I just didn't listen to it I lived it. I believed in the Ramones and Rock-n-Roll High school and I wanted to blow up my school too.

I saw my first rock concert at thirteen. It was The Fabulous Thunderbirds, ZZ Top and the Rolling Stones in the Houston Astrodome, What a life changing experience.

Between the ages of thirteen and fifteen I had made the progression from all my classic rock studies of the Beatles, Stones, Yard birds, Hendrix, Doors, and Led Zep, all the way through southern rock ZZ Top, Outlaws, Skynard, Molly Hatchet, Through punk rock with Sex Pistols, Ramones and The Clash, New wave with The Cars, Blondie, The Smiths, Ministry, Depeche Mode, and graduated to Heavy Metal and blues. I stole every book the library had on rock music or guitars and my room was one continuous poster.

The only close I owned were torn up blue jeans and T shirts of rock bands. I was a child prodigy and could play any song that I heard on guitar, bass or drums and

I was playing Iron Maiden, scorpions and Judas Priest in the eighth grade. I just understood music and I could feel it.

I listened to records every day and read rock magazines, emulating the dress and lifestyle portrayed by my Idols who I really considered peers that had gone before me. The most powerful people in the world were Rock stars and this was going to be my chosen profession and I needed to stop wasting my time in school and get on with my destiny. I loved Rock-n-Roll music and it has remained the voice of my people or tribe. As a teen punk rock and heavy metal were passionate vocal and expressive forms of art and a live rock concert was a surrealistic emotional and spiritual high.

A gathering of my people rejected by society and unified by rock-n-roll. Music is power and I understood the power of music.

I was introduced to marijuana at the age of thirteen. I had held off the temptation for several years, My brother smoked pot, my cousins smoked pot and were drug dealers, and one by one my peers started smoking. First Andy, then Thad, then Larry all in about a two week period. One night I spent the night with my friend Jimmy who had stole some pot from his mom. We both lied to each other about smoking before but soon confessed to each other when we were lying on the floor laughing our ass off and stoned for the first time. Boy did things change after that. By the end of that month I had tried marijuana, hashish, opium and mandrax and I had seen someone overdose on intravenous drugs. Not to mention that Thad's folks Ella and Jerry, who were like my second parents owned a liquor store and grandma Parker would let us sneak a bottle of whatever we wanted when we helped her stock the shelves. We wanted to be rock stars so we lived like one. I even dropped my first hit of acid in the seventh grade at the Rocky Horror Picture Show. Not only did this completely fuck up my since of sexuality but I was French kissed by a hot girl with a Mohawk that I didn't know while I was tripping my balls off and watching the movie. Kind of hard to go back to cheerleaders after that. I met that girl again about four years later and she remembered me, after that we were partners hanging out in Montrose for about six months. She's dead now; I think she died of aids.

I had stopped attending church because of the prejudices that now applied towards me. I had been unknowingly self medicating as a means to stabilize my illness and since everything I believed was wrong according to the church including Rock music, "I was a musician and loved rock music" girls "I had a beautiful girlfriend that I

was already having sex with and wasn't about to stop for Jesus" and smoking pot "which was the only thing that calmed me down or made me feel half way normal". For the next eight years I devoted my energies toward using my special powers or gifts to become a rock star and hating Christians. If God wouldn't love me because I was different then I was going to play for the other side. From the age of thirteen until I was twenty I smoked marijuana, and experimented with Cocaine, LSD, Opium, Hashish, Mandrax, mushrooms, Quaaludes, Rjs, Rj8's, Ecstasy , Crystal Meth and I was a teenage alcoholic. I worked to make money to buy equipment (drugs were almost always free when your popular and in a band),
I partied to increase my popularity and fame and I wrote music and played in bands. Everything that I did was geared towards fulfilling my destiny. I knew that if I worked hard enough that I would be an international Rock Star by the age of nineteen and this was my only goal.

CAPTER SEVEN
THE GIRL OF MY DREAMS AND
THE WOMAN OF MY NIGHTMARES

I had met my only girlfriend Athea when I was thirteen and in the eighth grade. I can still remember clearly the first time that I ever saw her beautiful face. She was the only girl that I ever dated or slept with and I considered her my wife, she was my soul mate and I intended to be with her forever. She is still today the most beautiful and special woman that I have ever known and my life is incomplete without her. Athea and her two sisters Cheri and Terra lived with their aunt Peggy and uncle Mike who owned a bar called Heartbreakers. Every day I would ride the school bus to Athea's house and stay there until her folks got home and then walk to Thad's or walk the full five miles home.
On weekends I would ride my bike and we would meet in the park. Where we would hold each other for hours and dream of the day that we could be together forever.
She was my girl and I was her man.
When I was sixteen years old my parents left Houston and moved to Austin, TX, I quit school so I could return to Houston to see Athea and jam with my friends. One weekend while jamming with my friend Mike English, we were discovered by a rock music producer and were invited into the studio to do some recording for a demo. We were hardly sixteen and could play dueling lead guitar solos. The very next day I was on my way to get some fresh guitar strings when Mike and I had a motorcycle accident and were laid up for six months. A woman driving a delivery truck pulled out in front of us and just stopped. I broke my left arm, left leg and crushed my left ankle. Mike who was on the back of the bike flew completely over the truck that we hit and landed on the other side sustaining only minor injuries bruised kidneys and ripped ligaments in his knees.
It was during the time of my recovery that Athea left me and ran off to New York with another man. He was a man much older than me and she married him to get away from her mother and her home life. His name was Jerry and he was abusive and unfaithful to her and treated her like shit but she was his girl now.

I was devastated! I could not understand it. I truly loved her and thought we were meant to be together forever. At seventeen years old I was completely suicidal and I suffered my first nervous or psychotic breakdown. Life basically meant nothing at all to me and this fueled my hatred towards God even more. I never dated another girl and I hated women from that time on.

CHAPTER EIGHT
SATAN'S PLAN REVIELED

Now I was living in Austin, the live music capital of the world and I had moved my friends Mike and Jimmy from Houston and teamed up with a bass player from Florida named Art Napoli and started a band called Texas Metal. Music was going through some changes at that time and we were playing everything from Metallica to Iron Maiden and from Rush to Megadeth as well as our own brand of hate fueled rebellious music. I felt as if I were trapped in Austin, until I met Art, we had a common vision and addiction and Art wanted to be a rock star too. I talked him into quitting school to practice every day and we played at our first Live Music festival called Wood Shock at seventeen years old.

I convinced my childhood friends Jimmy and Mike to leave home and join Art and I in our effort to take over the world. During this period of time we partied like rock stars. I played with this band and its consecutive offspring bands until I was kicked out of my own band for being too controlling and too wasted all the time.

It was like going through a divorce, I loved these guys and they just could not understand my drive and ambition and all rock stars were wasted, it was a prerequisite. At the age of nineteen I returned to Houston to work in the petrochemical industry and to put myself through music school.

By the time I reached the age of twenty I was living in a warehouse studio loft in Houston, still attending music school, teaching private guitar lessons and partying on the weekends.

One week end I went to an outdoor rock concert that I had seen advertised at the local liquor store. At the concert there were three friends of mine from school that had become born again Christians and had a Christian metal band. When I went backstage to visit them this evangelical guy named Chris Jenkins from a similar heavy metal background was trying to convince me that Satan had possessed my mind and body through heavy metal music and that the voices in my head were demons. I told him he was full of shit, that's when I had my first full blown audio hallucination where I heard the voice of God tell me that "I was un pure and that I was arguing with a child of God".

Well being completely freaked out by this experience I of course repented and joined a church the next day. When I explained to the pastors and clergy the background I had come from and that even though I had accepted Jesus and believed, I was still hearing the voices and the voices told me that Jesus wasn't real, They all jumped on me and started performing an exorcism and casting the demons out of me right there on the stage in front of everyone. They said that the reason the demons had such a strong hold on me was because of the special calling on my life and that I would need the help of the holy spirit to give me power over the demons, then gave me bible scriptures to back up all crap they were telling me. I bought it all hook line and sinker.

Well not wanting to be a pawn of Satan anymore and needing an answer for my talents, insight, abilities and obsessive drive as well as seeing visions and hearing voices, after all I had been in heavy metal bands and listened to Satanic heavy metal music, I had been wasted and hated Christians for eight years, so it was completely logical to believe that I was possessed by Satan. After all it was in the bible.

I received the gift of the holy spirit with the evidence of speaking in tongues (babbling a bunch of psychotic bullshit that doesn't mean anything) and was completely delivered from eight years drugs and alcohol. I not only believed that I had been tricked into serving Satan and doing his will, but that the feelings I had for Athea were born in sin and that the only reason that I wanted her was because she was the embodiment of beauty and carnal sin. So I stopped listening to all secular music and married the first Christian girl I met that was the complete opposite of Athea in every way. I married a nineteen year old former bar maid named Cindy with a four year old daughter named Danielle. I was happy and life was good for the next five years. Cindy and I had two children together Aaron and Natolie. Well with this new power, I found that through prayer and meditation in the scriptures and by babbling in tongues for hours I could occupy my mind and control the voices in my head or at least discern between the voice of God, the voice of the Spirit, my own mind and the voice of Satan. Now I had all the answers, I had super powers beyond that of mere mortals and I had become the Apostle Nathon Dees. During this time I was involved in a petrochemical plant explosion at work and received second and third degree burns on one fourth of my body including my face arm and chest. Since I had been delivered from drugs by Jesus I had to take a stand and make a testimony out of my life for other believers.

I refused to take any pain medication and I went through a month of de breeding and skin removal with no pain killer at all just praying and chanting in tongues while they exposed my nerve endings so new skin could grow. I had the powers of a shaman and could even control physical pain through my beliefs.

CHAPTER NINE
THE HOUSE OF CARDS COLLAPSES

How could I possibly be wrong? I made straight A's in seminary, I was a brilliant orator, I was successful, talented and people believed in me because I was called, set apart, recognized by my peers, licensed and ordained to preach the gospel, heal the sick, cast out demons, lead people to the kingdom of God and operate in the gifts of the spirit. I was completely delusional totally schizoaffective and on my way to the funny farm. I existed this way for nearly fifteen years before I was finally diagnosed as being mentally ill and woke up from the fairy tale land of Christianity. During this time I studied the bible day and night, went to devotionals, attended church every time the doors were open, stayed with the elders of the church performing exorcisms and casting out demons from people and holding independent bible studies in my home. When I wasn't doing this I was playing in an evangelical Christian rock band called Antidote and doing street ministry. My only purpose in life was to let people know about Jesus and deliver folks from hell.

This went on for five years before my first wife Cynthia backslid and went back into the world of alcoholism and partying. When Cindy left home I knew that it was time to file for a divorce. I didn't believe in divorce but I felt I had no option. If Cindy was going to turn her back on God she was an infidel. I was sure that I would get custody of Aaron and Natolie our two children and that I would get the house because I had the Kids. There was no way that I could possibly lose, I was in ministry, I was clean and sober, I was an outstanding member of the church, a

Free Mason, a business owner, and there was no way that I could lose in divorce court to a drunk and a whore that abandoned her children. I was wrong, I lost everything. I lost custody of my two children because I had a dick. I lost my brand new house that I had built myself and paid cash for because I did not have custody of the kids and I lost my faith because the only comfort that was offered to me by my pastor was "consider Job "a popular bible character that lost everything in a game between God and Satan to prove Job's loyalty to God. This sucked.

To make things worse the day that I was forced to leave my home and give up my children I asked God why this had to happen and he spoke to me audibly (another hallucination) and told me " It was not his will for me to be with Cindy but that in two years I would marry Athea". Well this made me furious with God. If I was meant to be with Athea then why did I have to endure this suffering and have my children with the wrong woman?

I knew that drugs and alcohol weren't the answer, I couldn't go back to the church. It was at this time that my old party buddy Bobby Daniels heard about what happened to me and felt like it was his duty to show me a good time. After five years of being clean and sober it only took one invitation to party from Bobby and I was out on the dance floor every week end wigging on X and completely free from God and Cindy and making plans to start a punk rock cult following.

CHAPTER TEN
A WAY OUT

I felt like I was out of control and needed to be institutionalized. I knew I would die from drug abuse if I started a band and I had no personal strength without Christ.

I needed a way to regroup and start over, I knew that if I didn't pull my shit together I would never receive custody of my children so at twenty five years old I enlisted in the US Army. I actually had to fight to get in the Army. I was a divorced twenty five year old white male with a GED and they didn't want me.

It was a great plan, in the Army I could pay my child support, get away from Cindy and I wouldn't need to worry about food or clothing, plus with a three year enlistment it was impossible for God's will to take effect concerning Athea because I was obligated to the government for a minimum of three years and I could stay away from drugs there. The first Day that I was in basic training I was pulled aside by a Pentecostal drill sergeant that had read my personnel file. He told me that I was there because God had a special plan for my life and that although I was mad at God he still loved me and had a special purpose for me. How could God find me here, I was running away from him. I got a job killing people so I could die in combat and make my children proud and my X wife suffer not so I could serve God. During this time I was completely manic, working with the chaplains corps and attending

Pentecostal church on Sunday and playing soldier while getting drunk every other night. I excelled in the Army earning two field grade promotions and four Army achievement awards in less than two years. I was on fire, I had a purpose again and I was institutionalized where all I had to do was meet or exceed a set standard and I would be recognized and rewarded.

During my stay at Fort Sill I had decided at one point that if I defaced my body that God would reject me from the calling and I would be free. At first I just pierced my nipple and my nose but not wanting to be a poser I soon committed to tattooing my skin which was a major sin. That's when I met my friend Rocky, he was a Christian biker tattoo artist that was a former president of the Vietnam Vets motorcycle club. Rocky told me the same thing that everyone else did, I was special and God had a plan for me and that right now I was just pissed off at God. Rocky taught me that I could be a Christian without being a dick. Meeting someone that I could respect from my world that was a Christian helped perpetuate my faith during my time of spiritual darkness.

After only "you guessed it" two years in the Army I woke up one morning expecting to hear from God, so I sat down and meditated with a pen and paper waiting to hear from God and I did. The audible voice of God spoke to me and told me that my time of isolation and rebuilding was over and that I was leaving the Army but not to worry about where I would go or what I would do because he was in complete control and that his will would be done in my life. The very next day my captain called me into his office and told me that I had lost my security clearance because the Army had found out that I had filed bank bankruptcy before enlisting in the Army and that I could reenlist with a new non secure MOS or that I could go home with a full honorable discharge and all my benefits.

I consulted with all my superiors and they all said the same thing. "PFC Dees you came here a broken man now you've rebuilt yourself, go home and start over because you can do anything you want and you're wasting your time here". Well that's not the speech I was expecting at all, but it was the truth so I left Fort Sill and went back to Austin to write and record a new album and start a band.

CHAPTER ELEVEN
BACK TO THE WITCHDOCTORS

While I was recording the album I would have periods of confusion where I could not think or concentrate because of the flood of thoughts going through my head, then I heard the word reprobate in my mind and remembered the scripture that said a double minded man was unstable in all his ways and would be given over to a reprobate mind. I thought that I was losing my mind and that I would go insane if I did not serve God. I made an appointment to see a pastor friend in Houston that was into demonic deliverance ministry and left Austin the next day.

When I got to Houston I had some time to kill so I went to my kids' school to meet their teachers and see how they were doing, that's when I found out that since the time that I left for the Army my X wife Cindy had gone completely out of control and that both of my children were being physically abused and neglected by their mother and that I had better make preparations to take custody of my children. Well I knew that Cindy and I didn't see eye to eye but I had no Idea that she had become a severe child abuser while I was in the Army. Well by this time I was pretty shook up by the whole ordeal and went on to my appointment with Brother Robert Pitts the Christian prophet to find out what was really happening to me. When I arrived at his house he was ready for me and told me that God had told him that I was coming and prepared him for the meeting. When I explained to him what was going on in my head and with my life, (basically explaining to him the symptoms of Schizoaffective disorder) he proceeded to explain how that I had allowed Satan to have a toe hold in my life through my rebellion towards God and how that I would need to go through complete demonic deliverance no matter what it took. After he called all the prayer warriors in the church he then called another pastor friend of his to join us and we drove to the church where they took me to their upper prayer room and started the exorcism. After repenting and renouncing and denouncing Satan and everything you could imagine these guys laid hands on me and blabbed in tongues and screamed at demons until my brain shorted out and I fell to the floor.

My third nervous or psychotic breakdown. Well hell after that I didn't hear any voices and if I did I surely wasn't going to tell these guys.

CHAPTER TWELVE
ATHEA AND THE SUPER CHURCH

Well now that I was cleansed and pure again I sure didn't want to get to far from the church and I needed to come up with a plan to fight for the custody of my children. I had one more thing that I needed to do, find Athea and tell her I was sorry for hating her for so long and that I forgave her.

I figured that I would go to her parents bar and see where I could find her.

I drove to her town and went to find her. I found her Aunt Peggy and told her I wanted to see Athea, she told me that Athea never came there anymore because she was a born again Christian and that if I wanted to see her I needed to go to The Abundant Life Christian Center in La Marque, TX so I visited the Wednesday night service hoping to see Athea who I had not seen in ten years.

This was a giant super church televised worldwide, there were thousands of people there and I didn't think I would find her there so I enjoyed the service and figured that God had some other reason for me to be there.

When the service was over I walked down the corridor on my way out disappointed not to see her, but glad I came; when there she was. It was the girl of my dreams standing there in a church, saved, born again, single and more beautiful than I could have ever imagined. This was the first time that I had seen Athea as an adult woman. I had always convinced myself that Athea's looks would deteriorate rapidly from the hard living and not to expect that much, after all she had two kids. I was wrong! She was absolutely exquisite. From her beautiful long hair cascading gently over her shoulders to her tall, slim perfectly molded body filling her mid length black dress. Her face was the face a girl I once knew sculpted into the Image of a Greek Goddess. She was once again the most beautiful woman that I had ever seen.

That night we went for coffee with her sister Cheri that had also been born again and I told them my saga and what I had been through that week. Cheri had just graduated from seminary at Abundant Life and Athea was enrolled for the next semester. The next day I returned to Austin packed up my goods and moved back to Houston were I took a job with room and board and enrolled myself in seminary.

I needed to be closer to my children so I could help them and so I could start developing a case against my X wife and eventually win custody of my children. I wanted to be closer to Brother Robert because he had helped deliver me from Satan so I apprenticed under him while I went to school with Athea. I was holding on to the promise that God have gave me that I would marry Athea in two years but I never told her what I believed, in addition Bro. Robert told me that God had spoke to him and that Athea and I would be wed.

We never dated, I never asked her out and all we did was go to church, study and let our children play together when I had weekend visitations with Aaron and Natolie.

"Out of everything that I have ever experienced in spiritualism I can now explain it through psychology and credit to my mental illness, all of the voices, all of the visions, the highs and the lows, the beliefs, everything; but there is one event that I will never be able to explain"

One night while attending seminary Athea and I were doing homework together and listening to Christian music and talking. I told Athea just in conversation that If I had a wife I would like to learn ball room dancing because I thought it would be cool to do something like that with your girl. She told that she had made an impossible list for God, one that no man could fulfill and that over the course of time that we had been together God had shown her one by one that I fulfilled everything on that list and that ballroom dancing was the last thing on the list.

I asked her to dance and this was the first time I had held her close or touched her in any intimate way since we had reunited. When I held her in my arms and started dancing I immediately felt my very being leave my body and enter into hers, go completely through her and return back into my body. At that very moment Athea pulled away from me startled and asked what just happened. She explained to me that at that instant she could not tell the difference between she and I, and she knew beyond any doubt that she was holding her husband. We were married on December 16, 1996 and with her two young sons Teagan and Haeden with us we started a new life and began building a child custody case to win the battle for Aaron and Natolie so our household could be complete. Just as a side note, at some point between the end of this chapter and the beginning of the next I was building custom cedar chest in my woodworking shop when a board got sucked into my table saw and I cut off the finger tips on my left hand. I actually heard the voice of God tell me to pick up my push board and I replied back " I'm Nathon Dees Master Craftsman" , "I can handle this" as the board sucked into the blade. I pushed the bloody nubs together and wrapped up my hand and packed it in ice and my brother Robert took my to three different hospitals until he found a surgeon that could sew them back on. Thanks Rob!

For years I had struggled with my pride being a musician, well that was over now. If I could ever even play again I would be happy. I remember Art telling me that the curse was broken and I was free from being a musician and could live a normal life now. It took me years to retrain myself to play and the fingers were never quite the same but I retained my virtuosity.

CHAPTER THIRTEEN
TAKING OVER THE WORLD

Athea and I both had issues to work out but as long as we had Jesus we would find a way. I was working as an associate pastor at Bro. Roberts' church and studying family law over the internet. Athea and I were living in the parsonage of the church and involved in ministry and our children full time. During this time I also had a vision from God " which pastors do" and I converted the youth department of the church and the gym which wasn't being used into the largest Christian teen club and espresso bar in the city of Houston, with live music every weekend as well as pool, foosball, darts, roller skating and a cool atmosphere for teenagers. I had moved my friends recording studio into the teen club and was on my way to being the one of the most influential people in the Christian rock music scene in Houston. I had bands booked from all over the state. After only a few months of operation there were more people visiting The Café Esprit "which I had named the club" than there were people attending church on Sunday. This would not do. The Church soon complained that the families coming on Friday and Saturday nights didn't attend our church but were from other churches and that some of the kids that were coming weren't Christians.

"NO DUUH, THAT WAS THE POINT DUMBASSES!"

The problem of my life, if you accomplish more than your superiors and it makes them look bad and you lose favor quickly. The Café Esprit ministry was taken away from me and given to someone else to run after accusations were made accusing me of having my own crazy agenda "like saving the lost" and I was forced to resign. All I could see was a lack of vision and complacency. If these people really believed in God, than nothing would be more important than reaching people for Christ and no vision was too big for God. The Café Esprit is still in operation today but it never fully accomplished what I had set out for it to do.

By this time I had filed for the child custody case Pro Se and Athea and I did all the case research ourselves. When I had finished doing my homework I had over 500 pages of reports from child protective services on abuse and neglect towards my children and eighteen police reports for domestic disturbances at my X wife's house. Aaron was in the third grade at this time and was sleeping in class and had a fifty percent grade average in school and was failing every subject. He was too intelligent to get a learning disability label and was labeled as having an emotional disorder. Athea tutored Aaron on Wednesday nights and weekends and brought him up to a B average in one semester and he passed the year on high test scores. I could see a carbon copy of myself in Aaron, only compounded by the fact that he had been physically abused by his mother and was involved in an ugly custody battle. We even found out that while I was in the service Cindy would leave the children at home alone for days at a time and that Aaron who was nine was caring for Natolie who was five. When Athea and I took the case to trial the evidence that we presented was so strong that we were given soul managing conservatorship of the children and Athea was made their legal mother. We also got my house back because Cindy didn't pay the taxes on it. As soon we won custody of the kids we sold the house, packed our bags and moved to Wimberley, Texas were I would design and build a 2400 sq ft house with five bedrooms , two and a half baths, a studio, two car garage and my beautiful wife and our four children. I thought the trouble was finally over and things were going to be easy now. I was making good money sometimes, we were living in our dream home that we built ourselves, Athea was home schooling all four children and running her massage business, while I built houses, put in septic systems, built a motel for my father and I owned

and operated a custom motorcycle shop with my old buddy Art who was still playing in bands and partying. I still had no Idea that I was anything less than anointed and ambitious, driven and motivated with a grand purpose for life as long as I could do enough to keep the forces of Satan from entering into my mind and destroying God's plan for my life. There was nothing that could stop me as long as I could discern the voice of Satan and follow the voice of God". We were as my friend Don Cool would say" Partridge Family Jesus Freaks " serving the Lord ministering to bikers, rehabilitating drug attics in our own home and serving faithfully in a local church, once again playing in the music ministry and doing demonic deliverance ministry on other mentally ill Christians.

CHAPTER FOURTEEN
THE DEVILS BACK IN TOWN

About the time of the 9/11 attack I was having problems with my marriage because Athea who is still a Christian, thought I didn't really love her for some reason. We could speak in tongues, hear the voice of God, see demons and angels how could Athea not know I was in love with her. Well this must have been the greatest Demonic attack of my life because neither God or the Holy Ghost would defend me in this matter and tell my wife the truth that I would have gladly laid down my own life for her. Sometimes I had trouble controlling my emotions but I was always faithful to my marriage and I loved my wife. Athea was the object of my every affection and fulfilled my every romantic fantasy so why would I want someone else?

Her own feelings of inadequacy and concepts of self value and worth which being bi polar and a man I could not possibly understand drove her to believe that no man could truly love his wife or at least I did not love her.

Well when she stopped having sex with me because I didn't love her well that was the straw that broke the camel's back. I was really cracking up over this and the thought of losing everything again when I had done nothing wrong only entered me into the "Holy Job" category again which I did not want to be in.

I was painting olive oil crosses on the doors and windows of the house, I was anointing my head with oil and walking the lengths of my property in the name of Jesus to prevent Satan from lying to my wife and I was slowly losing my mind. I saw demons around every corner and new Satan was destroying me through my wife once again.

The only way that I was able to deal with my intense sex drive was to be married. I was a good provider, a faithful loving and husband and father and was deeply and passionately in love with my wife. To deny me sex on the basis on infidelity was an insult to everything that I was and everything that I believed.

During this time of trouble my good friend Rabbi Bruce Abraham whom I respected a great deal gave me a joint of some really good marijuara and told me I had better smoke it and just chill the fuck out for a while or I was going to lose it for good. Bruce told me that I had lost touch with reality and that my wife was fucked up too.
I have found this to be very sound advice and good council. When I sat down in my back yard and smoked that joint, for the first time since I had been saved on Nov 11,1987, I realized that everything in my life was a complete lie if Athea did not know our love was real after what we had experienced together in the supernatural " the exchange of souls" and that if I truly believed the things I professed to believe as a Christian about demons controlling our thoughts and Satan destroying my marriage than I was a complete paranoid schizophrenic and that I was no different than the religious extremist Muslim kooks that performed the terror acts of 9/11. This was either the most enlightening event of my life or Satan had complete control of my mind. My wife, along with my friends and peers in the church said that this was an attack from Satan or attributed it to the pot but I knew clearly by this time that I had wandered out of my Jesus box and I knew too much to ever go back in.

CHAPTER FIFTEEN
RUN AWAY, RUN FAR AWAY FAST

I needed to find out the truth once and for all so in a classic bi polar move I divorced the girl of my dreams (who didn't believe I loved her any way), closed my business, sold and gave away everything that I had, took my two kids and moved to a beach on the pacific coast of Costa Rica far away from everyone and everything.
Here I would find out once and for all what was real and what was not. During this time period I did a lot of soul searching and inner healing dealing with hating my wife and hating Christians. Still completely delusional undiagnosed and untreated and without religion to protect me from myself I partied my ass off, surfed, swam, played guitar and tried to come up with a new purpose or plan. I had lots of new non Christian Friends and I got to play music a lot and pot was legal, cheap and plentiful. I wanted to meet someone new but knew that the chances of ever finding someone as wonderful as Athea would be next to impossible and I wasn't about to settle for less.
I decided to open another teen club but this time without interference from the church. I would create a safe place for Costa Rican kids to hang out and teach my new doctrine called " Pull your head out of your ass" which was based on principles of common sense without the use of religious fear and nirvana manipulation to get the point across. I leased a building and completely built out a live music venue with an espresso bar, stage, lights, sound system and a restaurant. Nathon's Place was completely finished and all I was waiting for was

my operating permit. That's when I found out that I had leased a building that had been built illegally and could not be permitted. The guy who owned the building knew there were problems with the city but thought he would have the issues resolved before I found out that he was a liar and a thief and had stole my money. I lost nearly thirty thousand dollars and six months of work.

On top of everything else that could have went wrong, my brother Evil Damon had been released from prison and my father thought he just needed a new start too so he broke Damon's parole and illegally smuggled him into Costa Rica. All he wanted to do "he said" was move far away into the mountains and disappear. It took less than two weeks for him to be a complete lunatic crack head running the streets of my new home town stealing from people and causing trouble. I had once again been sold out by my dad and linked to this blood sucking criminal just because he was my brother. I hated Damon and left the country to get away from this piece of shit in the first place.

After nine months of effort to start a new business and life in Costa Rica everything I had tried fell through for one reason or another and now my brother who I hated and feared was here with me. I soon suffered another nervous breakdown.

CHAPTER SIXTEEN
THE CRASH LANDING BACK HOME

I was broke and hopeless and ready to go home. I had a new explanation and mission when I returned to the US, I was still an apostle, but God had called me out of the church because I had been chosen to bring the light of God to non Christians and stand in direct opposition to the false Christian church and their lying doctrines. I went back to the states and started a nonprofit association and started counseling people in the community with two other pastor friends Mike Klumpp and Steve Townsend that had been excommunicated by the church for not agreeing with mainstream Christian doctrine.

Both Mike and Steve were licensed ministers and counselors. Mike is the author of The Single Dads Survival Guide, a martial arts expert and a biker. Steve is the president of the Alliance Motorcycle ministry, he is the official Chaplin over every outlaw motorcycle club in Central Texas and is on the board of directors of the Confederation of Clubs in Texas.

Mike is the first person that diagnosed me as being Bi Polar one night while we were talking about our clients and then Steven told me that he was Bi Polar too.

During this time I was again completely manic and making all kinds of things happen, I had reunited the children with their mother and was helping to rehabilitate my X wife Cindy, I built a miniature golf course and BMX bike track and opened it free for kids in the community and I was writing and recording an album of anti Christian hate music that God had inspired me to write while I was in Costa Rica.

I was running all of my father's business while he was in Costa Rica dealing with Damon. During this time I was also getting a band together to take the truth of God to my people the bikers, skaters, surfers and rock n rollers the people that had not bought into the lies of Christianity. I was getting ready to take over the world and willing to die for what I believed was true. Then things went sour again. Cindy started drinking again and Aaron got busted for pot at school and Damon was expelled from Costa Rica For the first of many times. I had all of the influences from society in the US, all the churches and all my Christian friends waiting for me to be delivered from Satan once again and my beautiful wife Athea whom I already had plans to remarry, speaking in tongues and claiming our marriage in the name of Jesus (God finally told her that I really loved her) and praying for me all the time and trying to suck me back into the delusional lies of Christian faith. Well between that, my business, my investments in Costa Rica and my new found anti Christian faith and the return of my fugitive brother. I suffered my final nervous or psychotic break down to date.

That is when I finally put down my theology books and started studying psychology for an answer.

CHAPTER SEVENTEEN
LOOSING MY RELIGION

I had studied the bible for years just learning how to decipher its meanings and languages so I could understand the truth, It only took one week of research for me to completely understand what was happening to me, where it came from and how long it had been effecting my life.

First I went to the book store and bought a book on surviving bi polar disorder since that was my obvious goal. After reading this book and researching RH Factor and schizophrenia on the internet I knew way more than I wanted to know. Next I needed to have a greater understanding of some of the subject matter I was reading so I went to a Goodwill store and bought a med school Psychology book for five dollars took it home and read it from cover to cover. Then I started hitting libraries and researching schizophrenia. It was real, it was proven, it was science and most of all didn't require faith to believe.

I was mentally ill, had been for a long time and I had gone as far as I could go.

Then I went a step farther and got some books that were taboo to the church and I studied philosophy and its origins completely laying out the history of modern thought and the birth of religions and even their purposes. I still wasn't quite sure if I would still need to confront Satan or not so I bought a book called The Exhaustive Encyclopedia of Demonology and witchcraft.

I would carry this book around just to see the fear in people's faces when they asked what you were reading. I had studied Satanism, the occult, witchcraft and pagan religion in the church and new a great deal about the dark side but this book was not what I expected. It was just what it said it was an encyclopedia. A chronological life time study in alphabetical order of the history of Satanism, witchcraft and demonology.

This book made the Foxes Book of Martyrs "required reading for all Christian seminary students" look like a stroll in the park. There was no way to compare what other people did to Christians against what Christians did to other people. When I read what people believed and did throughout the history of Christianity after they created Satan and his demons to manipulate people with fear I understood that I was a part of a nearly two thousand year old lie.

The rituals practiced in the dark ages by Christian witch hunters were the same exact same theories and practices that had been applied to me and that I had applied to others. The arts of exorcism and demonic deliverance were developed during this 1800 year old Christian practice of hunting down and killing witches. The text that the church used to establish the doctrines of the dark crafts where written by men that were writing instructions for the persecution of anyone practicing the dark crafts and instructions on torturing and killing witches.

The rest of the doctrine was established by the testimony of the innocent people that confessed under severe torture and were murdered any way. Being one of the few Christians eaten by lions would have been a pick-nick compared to what open courts sanctioned and ruled by the church did to millions of men women and children in the name of Jesus.

I had become so delusional as a Christian that I was performing mid evil psychology on myself my family and my friends. I was using the same lame pathetic unrealistic theories that these assholes in the book used to kill people from about two hundred AD until the witch hunts of Salem. Satanism was created by Christianity and the two had to co exist. Christianity is a fear/reward based doctrine designed to manipulate the simple and the mentally ill. It's all inclusive unless you're a fag or you're just not stupid enough to believe it. I thought Satan was out to kill me because the bible said so and the bible was true.

I believed in demons because they were in the bible. I thought psychology was the enemy of god because it said that normal people prayed and even had faith but only mentally ill people are able to hear or see metaphysical beings. The bible says if you can't hear my voice you must not know me.

Hell everyone in the bible hears voices and sees metaphysical beings and we all know that God's word is forever and never changes so it must be true for today.

Well Mr. Bi Polar book and the DSM-IV says that if you hear voices it is a symptom of mental illness and this book isn't two thousand years old, it's cutting edge medical technology covering years of scientific research and data. This book says if you see visions, you are hallucinating and you should try some Risperdone. The bible talked about transcendence and out of body experiences. Well so did the psychology book and by the time that I understood the depth of schizophrenia I was glad just to be Schizoaffective. I had all the symptoms of severe juvenile onset Chronic rapid cycling Bi Polar one disorder and young adult schizophrenia with mixed episodes and I had them for a long, long time.

I could have never been properly diagnosed as long as I was a Christian because I would have even considered the questioning during the diagnoses as being anti Christian and trying to devalue my beliefs. Only unbelievers didn't believe what the bible said and I did see devils and angels, and I could hear the voice of God.

I was the Rev, Nathon Q, Dees and the only way that I could accept something that was actually going to destroy my very identity, I was going to need to be born again, again.

This time born of the flesh not of the spirit and grounded in secular reasoning. No metaphysics, if it's not physical don't take it for granted that it is real or that it's even there. No concepts of an afterlife but a greater understanding of life itself. No more alternate realities, the most real fact I could understand was that I was severely mentally ill and I had eluded treatment by entering into a fantasy world where my symptoms were perfectly normal, totally acceptable and even admired and encouraged. In fact my life has now become completely useless because I have lost the ability to believe and dream. I don't want to get sucked into another cult or a messed up relationship just because I want to achieve the delusion of being happy when happiness itself is only a concept derived from teachings, experiences and beliefs.

CHAPTER EIGHTEEN
IS SIGMOND IN THE HOUSE?

By the time I finished my research I knew for a fact that I was mentally ill and had been the whole time. This was the third time I had went to a doctor for mental and emotional issues but it was the first time that I had educated myself enough to know that science was not the enemy of God and was prepared to accept the diagnoses. Since I had diagnosed myself and I had done a tremendous amount of research on the science of mental illness I was looking for a confirmation and boy did I get one.

Three different mental health professionals concluded that I did in fact have extreme Schizoaffective disorder and that my sixteen year old son had it too. One doctor said that it was unbelievable that I had never been hospitalized for my condition and wanted to know how that I could have possibly survived so long without medical treatment. "The answer was easy" I told him, I was a right wing charismatic Christian and in fact a pastor involved in demonic deliverance ministry and that all of my hallucinations both audible and visual as well as my emotional problems and mania were perfectly acceptable in Christian doctrine and better yet even validated the gifts of my calling. I had been institutionalized with a lot of other mentally ill people using mid evil psychiatry to explain away our mental and emotional problems and the largest support group of idiots in the world to back me up and a bible to prove it. Then I was institutionalized in the Army were all I had to do was follow orders and be extreme which I was good at, they told me everything I needed to know. I knew what to wear, when to eat, what to say and had a complete itinerary of things to do each day. Finally I had been institutionalized in marriage, as long as I could bring home a pay check and stay erect I was OK. I had a full time nurse taking care of me as long as I was married. My clothes were washed my children were cared for and I didn't need to worry about sex. It was when Athea and I separated that I realized that I knew what I was supposed to do but I just couldn't do it. I was afraid of money and as long as someone else paid all of my bills I just needed to focus on making more money.

When I start doing finance, I start devaluing my own existence to the point that I hate very concept of money and wish that I lived in a communal society of craftsmen and farmers that traded goods amongst themselves. Some people like money and some people are good with it, I hate it and I'm either afraid to spend it or I invest it recklessly. Don't get me wrong I know how to make money and I've made lots of it. It is the concepts of value or self worth being attached to a trade or job and your overall value as a human being judged by how many dollars you can trade for hours and what sacrifices are you willing to make to have stuff. I had never really had to pay a bill in my adult life. I always had someone else to take care of the details for me.

CHAPTER NINETEEN
STARTING OVER AS A MORTAL

By this time I had lots of good answers but I was broke, homeless and trying to decide what was next for me now that I wasn't an apostle and I had wasted fifteen years of my life in the church when I could have been getting help, counseling and treatment for mental illness instead of running around completely out of my mind fighting demons, talking to angels and promoting this kind of insanity to others. I felt so guilty and ashamed, I felt lied to and molested, I had been diagnosed years before and chose to believe Gods word instead of trained and educated healthcare professionals.

I was attending psychiatric outpatient care at my local MHMR, having both my children screened and counseled while trying to adjust to five kinds of new medications. I was by myself with no support because all my friends and wife refused to believe that I was mentally ill because of the effect that it would have towards their own beliefs. Every time I passed a church I was angry and every time I heard their unrealistic bible based bullshit I just wished they could accept my illness and start supporting me, but no Christian could ever accept a pastors willing decision to choose Hell and a life separated from God and heaven for a diagnoses of mental Illness.

When I left the church after fifteen years of faith and service to the cross, I was so mentally ill that I applied for some financial aid and after a psychiatric review and an explanation of my former Christian Beliefs, I was given full social security benefits for being completely mentally disabled and no longer able to work or function in society.

I returned to Jaco, Costa Rica where I live in a surfer hostel by the beach and protect myself and my son from the good intentions of others. I stay completely out of contact with the Christian world I once knew and segregate myself from the Christian Nation of my home land.

In Costa Rica the evangelical movement didn't really go over and the people did not let the Catholic church mandate the rules of society, so for the most part it is a secular society where Christianity is not shoved down your throat.

Now days I'm just a mentally ill person struggling to survive day to day without having to be institutionalized. I smoke pot to stabilize the affects of my illness (which I can not do in the US) and try to take my medications, but sometimes they are worse than the illness, I walk up and down on the beach each day and sometimes go to the mountains and just look at the jungle, I have no real future now so I just try to enjoy life and I don't do much thinking about God or any metaphysical theologies that can induce psychosis. Although I live in paradise I still fight severe depression, anxiety, fear and even thoughts of suicide, but I am no longer tormented by imaginary demons from hell and I'm not killing myself and wasting my life trying to get to heaven.

CHAPTER TWENTY
WHAT ABOUT THE MUSIC

Music was always a major player in this whole religious experience. Next to being with Athea or knowing God it was my greatest passion. I was very talented and music came to me easy. In schizophrenia as well as Bi Polar disorder the presence of brilliance comes in the form of mania and almost like an idiot savant music is second nature at times and it flows like pure logic and can totally consume you. It is a free flowing expression of inner feelings, thoughts and beliefs capable of identifying lifestyles, cultures, creeds and religions. Music was the most powerful force in the world and I was God's chosen oracle to speak through. When I played lead guitar in church it was if I would go into a state of trance and just start ripping improvisational leads over the Christian music that was being performed. When my solo was finished I would open my eyes to find the whole church Raising their hands to God and praising him. Some times when I played the whole crowed would start running around the church and freaking out, rolling on the floor, jumping up and down like punk rockers and speaking in tongues. This was an incredible performing experience to say the least. When I played my guitar God was speaking to his people through the music and I was his voice.

This was in fact the very reason that Satan Hated me and wanted me dead. You see as a teenager I had made a covenant with Satan to make me a Rock Star if I served him. Satan had used me for a puppet to distribute his lies and send people to hell and I was good at it. I was the Apostle Nathon Dees and I had been sent to earth as a messenger to be a light in a world of darkness and lead God's people out of the bondage that I had been ensnared in. Even when I played for Satan people still recognized my supernatural gifts and were drawn to me as a charismatic leader and wanted to be a part of my vision. Well with this war going on it was easy to understand that all musicians or muses were created to glorify God and lead his people in praise and worship.

Every musician that used his gifts for secular purposes was either willingly or unwillingly using his or her gifts for the promotion of Satan's Army and to keep people from the light of God.

Some musicians were willing and faithful servants of Satan and received great rewards here on earth for their service. Fame fortune and Glory even if it was only for a limited time. Other musicians chose to give their glory to God and humble themselves to a life of service to the music ministry and a reward in heaven. Leading God's people in super natural worship.

It was a sin to use your talents and gifts for the world. Music was supernatural and it was created to occupy your mind and heart with the praises of God in worship. Music was the most intimate form of worship and the ultimate expression of faith and love towards God. Every successful secular Rock artist had at some point made a choice to serve Satan. The greater their influence on the people the greater their reward would be here on earth. I was in competition with secular artist for the souls of the lost. I felt as if I owed it to God to use my music to spread the name of Jesus to the lost and I would pay God back one hundred fold to redeem myself from serving Satan. This battle for my soul and talents started at age thirteen and continued until I was thirty six.

I had been in a constant tug of war between God and Satan over my gifts and there was no middle ground I was either on one side or the other. Satan would play the secular music that I loved in my head while I was talking to God and I would have to pray in tongues and rebuke Satan in the name of Jesus until the music would go away and I could here only Christian music in my head. Any time that I was not actively involved in something there was a running conversation in my head between God, Satan and the Holy Spirit. This conversation could take place twenty four hours a day forever if I let it. The voices would argue with each other about scriptures or events and failures in my life. I had to judge every thought that entered my head against my knowledge of the bible to see if the thought was from God or Satan. Satan had deceived the whole world into believing his lies and I was not going to let him take me down again.

This was completely acceptable behavior and is taught as Christian doctrine in your local church. This war inside my head and the constant struggle against the forces of darkness stood as the evidences of my calling and a sign of my spiritual gifts. I was completely delusional, out of my fucking mind and a very successful evangelical Christian minister with a powerful music ministry. The church loved me.

I possessed the ability to make things happen. We were at war and I was a soldier of God. Every decision that I made was in fact a life or death decision for some ones eternal soul. I possessed a divine gift of understanding and I got things done. That linked to good looks, talent, charisma and a beautiful wife and kids, hell who wouldn't want me on their team. I was supernatural officer material and I had worked my way up through the ranks rapidly. I was already making plans to start my own church and learning how to do it from men with million dollar ministries.

You might say "hey you're a smart guy, how could you really believe all of that stupid shit?". All I had to do to maintain this completely delusional train of thought was read the bible continuously and go down to my local Christian book store. Here at the Christian bookstore you can find thousands of books written by thieves, liars and mentally ill people. Schizophrenics and scam artist writing books on everything from speaking in tongues and demonic deliverance, to hearing and understanding God's voice.

You see I had done a tremendous amount of research and all of the extreme doctrines I believed in were from books that I had read written by very powerful and influential teachers in the Christian church. Names like Jerry Falwell, John Osteen, Walter Hallam, Kenneth Copeland, Kenneth Hagen, Oral Roberts, Jesse Duplantus, Joyce Myers, Creflo Dollar, Benny Henn and many more.

These were all very powerful and successful pastors with worldwide ministries that conclusively are either liars and thieves that are out to make money off of people or they are delusional mentally ill people that should be removed from their powerful and influential positions for the good of mankind.

CHAPTER TWENTYONE
STOP AND THINK ABOUT IT

A delusion is defined as a false personal belief based on incorrect inference about external reality and firmly sustained despite of what everyone else believes and despite what constitutes incontrovertible and obvious proof or evidence to the contrary (DSM -IV, p.765)
If you are hearing voices and seeing visions chances are you are suffering from some form of mental illness or you are on some good drugs. Not spiritual enlightenment and world domination but a nice padded cell and some lithium for starters to stabilize your mania. I had always been taught that science was the enemy of God and now I understand clearly that religion is the enemy of counseling and therapy as well as timely and proper diagnoses of the mentally ill.
God does not audibly speak to people and there are no such things as angels or demons these are myths perpetuated by the lies of Christian Doctrine and exist only in the minds of believers. Separate yourselves from the delusional and insane and come out from among the deceitful and the deceived. Get the help you need and replace religious lies with medicine, counseling and facts.
The psychology behind Christianity is very extreme and the fact that so many people are so desperate for purpose and belonging or even social acceptance is absolutely amazing. It is a quite simple concept that if we are void of hope we find ourselves hopeless.
Hope in itself can be as simple as having a positive or hopeful attitude. In extreme or seemingly hopeless situations we can combine hope with faith which allows us to discount the natural and believe that the supernatural will take place.
Faith in God through Jesus gives us not only the hope that we might succeed in this life but offers us a second chance in the afterlife if we uphold the laws and practices that govern a religious based society or as it's referred to "The Kingdom of God on earth". You are born of flesh and are subject to the sin nature of flesh from birth and thereby condemned to hell, a hopeless situation, but through the death of the savior Jesus you can be redeemed from the curse of sin and saved from the torment of hell.

The grandiose delusion of heaven just isn't enough to persuade some people to join the church so the concept of hell was created and our adversary the devil was invented to manipulate people through fear into doing what was deemed as right and moral behavior. The problem with this Christian Nirvana/Damnation doctrine is that it establishes a course of action were there can be no truly self less act of Christian compassion because every action is motivated by reward or damnation. It is the equivalent of love enforced with a hand gun. It's kind of like marriage.

A covenant enforced by law and not love at least not unconditional love or God would make amnesty for all and not just those who accept his son. The problem is that amnesty for all would not leave a motivational factor for forcing people to do good and abstain from evil.

I can't even imagine what kind of constant stumbling block religion must create for mental health care professionals when they are trying to establish a working reality with a patient, if everything that the patient believes is a well documented lie with millions of followers to back it up. You have to give up heaven to get help.

When one becomes born again one creates an alternate reality in which you become a metaphysical spiritual being inside of a mortal body fighting against the mind will and emotions of man which are the enemy of God through the help of another metaphysical being the Holy Spirit. This is made possible because Jesus "God's Son" died on a cross and defeated Satan "the arch enemy of God" conquering sin in the flesh which allows you to become one with God through his Spirit.

These simple concepts alone are enough to signify insanity and one would need to be either completely ignorant or mentally ill to embrace such foolish and mid evil theories. Christian concepts like your mind and flesh being evil are no less than Spiritual Terrorism perpetuated by cruel and inhumane people.

Christianity condemns the entire world to death and subjects us to the daily crucifixion of our flesh to obtain self righteousness.

Christianity teaches us that the world only offers the lust of our eyes and flesh and the boastful pride of life and convinces us that we should trade our walk on part in the world and life for the afterlife in heaven and that our only purpose is to serve God.

CHAPTER TWENTY TWO
NEVER UNDERESTIMATE THE POWER
OF STUPID PEOPLE IN LARGE GROUPS.

Just being present in a atmosphere of people motivated by a common cause is a powerful force. From Amway to Hitler anyone who has ever experienced a large gathering orated by charismatic speakers has felt the power of acceptance or the experiential enlightenment of being a part of something more powerful than one's self. In a giant crowed full of people it is easy to be swept away in the emotional environment and make irrational decisions concerning faith and finance.
Eat shit, ten million flies can't be wrong.
If this whole Christian thing is about being loved, God sure asks for a lot in return. Love should be a balanced free flow of emotions flowing without inhibition or fear, towards someone or something, inspired by an inner emotional context of joy, elation or happiness and should be self motivated and a choice.
You should have the option of accepting or rejecting it but you can only be in it if you make a conscious choice to partake in it. The concept of being loved by God is an overwhelming idea to a hurting world of people wanting to be loved.
Well being loved by God shouldn't cost you your eternal soul if you did have one. God's love would be transcendent and present in all of creation flowing together in a universal oneness and harmony through the love of God for all. God's love shouldn't be a quest for world domination through evangelism using fear to manipulate people into a relationship. Nor would God's love require membership in a sectarian cult that's longing for the destruction of mankind so they can finally be segregated from the infidels and unbelievers and live in Nirvana for eternity with God while the unbelievers burn in hell with Satan. Let's not forget the other love of God where believers are sucked up into heaven and trained to kill and return to earth with Jesus to slaughter all the unbelievers left on earth.

Who needs that kind of love? That kind of thinking is insane.
Co dependant relationships with spiritual super beings that are hell bent on universal domination and the torture and destruction of all unbelievers in Hell in the name of love is pretty fucking weird if you think about it!!!

I'm only so mentally ill, I could only believe this horse shit for about fifteen years before I came to the realization that no rational individual with an education could ever accept these ancient myths as anything other than folklore and legend perpetuated by fear and ignorance.

To a Christian the concepts of an alternate reality are perfectly acceptable because they are already living in one. They feel shame because of the guilt imposed on them by a religious society and culture. There is a penalty for all those that fall short of the mandates of acceptable behavior and laws of their religion and therefore a need for redemption and forgiveness. Unfortunately to maintain this created reality of quasi holiness through redemption and forgiveness you must be brainwashed into believing the full content of Christian doctrine and belief including but not limited to the existence of :

SATAN: The former choir of leader of heaven who is now the King of Darkness after leading a rebellion against God and being cast down to be the evil ruler over the earth. He wears red pajamas and has a pitch fork.

Angels: Nine foot tall transparent warriors of light that work for God. Not pretty ladies or fat babies with wings

Demons: Fallen angels taking hideous forms that do the bidding of Satan their master and can inhabit humans and control their thoughts.

Witches: Humans that invoke the powers of Satan through the black arts or witchcraft. Both white and black magic.

Sorcerers: Much like the witches but more powerful and using the arts of sorcery for their magic.

Prophets: People chosen by God and given divine gifts of insight and prophesy and possess the ability to hear God's voice and cast out demons.

Curses: Evil words spoken over you that have power over your life.

Ancestral Curses: Curses imposed by God on entire families for generations.

Demonic Possession: Having your body play host to the spiritual embodiment of a demonic being that controls your thoughts or actions.

Faith healing: Believing that in the name of Jesus you can lay hands on the sick and they will recover.

Speaking in tongues: Possessing a spiritual language that Satan can't understand so that your spirit can send un hindered prayers to God and a supernatural gift that allows you to speak to people in languages that you don't know or understand.

Immaculate Conception: That Jesus is the only creature in the history of the planet, plant or animal that was ever conceived without a physical seed of it's own species being present and germinating.

Out of body experiences: Being removed from the physical body defying time, space, matter and gravity as you are either transported to another place, time or world or astral planning until you return to your body.

Resurrection: The re incarnation of inanimate dead human tissue into living breathing flesh. To bring the dead back to life.

Heaven: A spiritual Disneyland For Christians where you hang out forever and do nothing.

Hell: A land of molten lava and fire where you are tortured by Satan for not choosing to believe in Jesus no matter how good you were.

Now that you have accepted all of that all you need to do is understand the existence of a triune Godhead consisting of a father a son and a holy spirit which is the blueprint for the triune make up of man consisting of the body, spirit and soul which is the mind will and emotions of man.

If you can honestly say that you believe all that crap then you need to go to heaven and the church deserves ten percent of your income.

It seems as if it would be illegal to use Spiritual Terrorism to molest people's minds and suck them into a cult. Why aren't Christians subjected to the war on terror, they have the same twisted agenda as the people they are fighting. What is the difference, If I were blown up by a suicide bomber or if I were brainwashed and held hostage by a cult of radical religious extremist for fifteen years?

If I approached you on the street with a hand gun and threatened your life unless you accepted my belief or joined my quest for world domination than you might think you were in Nazi Germany and if you were a White nationalist during the time of Hitler you might even join enthusiastically.

Instead of a gun I'm going to approach with the number one selling book in history and claim that is Holy and inspired by God and that if you refuse to accept what this book has to say you will be condemned to hell for all of eternity and a social outcast here on earth living under the curse of sin. I would then began to explain to you how that you were a piece of shit unworthy of God's love because you were a sinner born of the flesh and that you were completely hopeless without God and I would explain that it didn't matter if you were a good person or not you were going down and that you would burn right next to murderers and pedophiles, rapist and criminals in hell for eternity if you chose not to believe what I believe.

That is Fucking Spiritual Terrorism and it is cruel and inhumane to sell these lies to mentally ill people looking for help. Trapping them with fear and then sucking out their money as they lure them towards heaven. We really can't afford to get rid of Christianity because it would soon be replaced by one of the other even worse religions and we would be pushed further back into the dark ages. It seems as if religion is a necessary evil almost like a divine military state forcing the masses into morality.

If Christianity were to be recognized for the Spiritual Terrorist group that they are, sucking people into their cult by brainwashing them through fear and manipulation, then as their leader Jesus was tried by a world tribunal for the atrocities committed by his cultic followers then I would in turn be tried as a war criminal just like the Nazis that believed in Hitler and were just following their orders. With the exception that history will reflect that Hitler was responsible for far less deaths than Jesus or Christianity in their two thousand years of murder and deception and it's not over yet. Idol worshiping spiritual cults in your home town. Churches performing rituals, baptisms, séances, laying on hands, faith healings, spiritual mapping, speaking in tongues and demonic deliverance and instead of a star of David, a swastika, pentagram or square and compass their symbol is a murder weapon, the cross of Jesus. Christian doctrine teaches that idolatry is witchcraft and an abomination to God, but the single most exploited cultic symbol of idolatry in the world is the murder weapon used by Christians as a pagan symbol of their faith. The presence of this cultic idol worshiping symbol is so prevalent in the US that I had to go to another country where I was not constantly subjected to the symbols of Spiritual Terrorism and to live without the constant reminder of the last fifteen years I had spent as a mentally ill hostage held prisoner by the lies of Christianity.

CHAPTER TWENTY THREE
WHAT'S LIFE LIKE NOW?

Here is where I am now. Back when I was in the states I was seeing a psychiatrist every two weeks, trying to come up with a cocktail of anti psych drugs that would stabilize my condition. I didn't attend any counseling for my condition because I understood perfectly what was happening and why. That made me a level three patient. Therapy and counseling were designed to help people understand and deal with what was happening to them. I had already discovered the answers on my own. Sitting around talking about things wasn't really going to help me much. I had been giving people counseling for years and I knew perfectly well what was up.

Reality Reconstruction Therapy.

What I needed to do was create an alternate reality where I could survive and take care of my children without being institutionalized. First I needed to remove the stressors that cause the anxiety, mania and psychosis. To do this I had to remove myself from the fast paced American culture and the Judeo/Christian society. No churches no Christians and far enough away from Athea that she would have to come find me this time and prove once and for all that she was totally committed to our love and to acknowledge the fact that we were both mentally ill. No more car or insurance or electric bills or pressure to be anything other than a mentally ill person. I moved back to Jaco, Costa Rica where I don't even know what day it is most of the time. I live in a tropical paradise where the mountains meet the ocean. If retiring in a tropical paradise is the greatest thing you can achieve in life then I'm not a failure after all because I'm here and you're not.

I had already lived in Costa Rica for nine months the year before and I knew that to live in Costa Rica legally all that I needed was a six hundred dollar a month US pension check to have pensionado residency. To get this pension I needed to apply for SSDI at the social security office. The qualifications for receiving the pension were that you must have paid into the social security program for at least five years within the last ten years, I had that.

You needed to prove that you had not been able to support yourself for over a year and have others that could sign an affidavit that they helped care for and support you during this period, I had that.

Most of all you needed to prove that you were permanently disabled and could no longer perform the task or trade that you had in the past and could not be retrained. Well by the time I got to this point I was so messed up on the meds they were giving me for the mental illness that I could hardly function at all. I had a diagnoses from the HMMR psychiatrist, from my local doctor and from the Veterans administrations psychiatrist and I knew a great deal about my condition so when the day came for my psychiatric review from the social security doctor I passed with flying colors and my statement didn't call for any review dates. I was permanently mentally disabled for life. They gave me eight hundred dollars a month for me and two hundred dollars a month each to my two children until they reached eighteen years old. Of course this was only enough money to live in absolute poverty in the US but in Costa Rica It was more than enough money to live comfortably and it was perfectly legal.

The day that I got my first pension check I went and got the words SCHIZOAFFECTIVE DISORDER 295.7 tattooed on my left fore arm inside of a yellow warning sign. This was my statement to the world "leave me alone, it's over, don't follow me I'm not the messiah I'm mentally ill. I finally once and for all knew who and what I was and had a government seal of approval. The tattoo also stands as a constant reminder not to try and be normal or have a life or a girlfriend or goals or ambitions because I'm fucked up and I can never win.

The most I can ever be is a mentally ill person that is subject to delusion. Jaco is a two mile stretch of beach surrounded by volcanic formed mountains that flow into a lava reef at each end. On one side jungles and mountains on the other side a popular surfing beach on the pacific shoreline.

Here in Jaco all I have to do is survive from day to day. It's not even like a real town in some ways, it's more like a carnival or amusement park for tourist, surfers and back packers. More and more wealthy outsiders keep showing up and exploiting this little town.

I think that in one or two more years Jaco will become the Las Vegas of Central America. There are eight new condominiums under construction at this time and real estate has become like gold. I will stay here as long as I can and then move on to the next surf village. During the high season there are thousands of visitors here from all over the world and I meet new people all the time. It's a party town with a festive flare. Gambling and prostitution are legal here and you can smoke all the pot that you want and no one cares. Almost all of us ex pats are alcoholics because it's easy to sit around and drink all day when you don't have to work anymore.

I live here with my dad and we run a surfers hostel on the beach. Having schizophrenia sometimes makes running a hostel the hardest thing I've ever done. Sometimes I get afraid of people and I don't want to meet any one new. Every time I meet someone they want to know my story, then they can't believe that I'm mentally ill or they feel awkward. If they are rock-n-rollers or stoners they usually understand and admire me for escaping the US and surviving my illness.

Like most Bi Polar musicians and artist I don't take my meds if there is any way I can avoid it. I hold off taking my anti psychotics until I hear voices telling me to kill myself. When the voices come I take lots off sleeping pills and I take Risperdone. When I wake up the next day there are no more voices. I am so used to having suicidal voices in my head that we make a running joke about me killing myself.

It's just like fighting demons but now I know that the demons are me. They are random messages of self destruction created by my mental illness. They can come on at any time and for any reason but all you have to do is not agree with them. You don't argue with the voices you just don't agree after all it's just bad brain signals. I don't date or go out and I don't sleep with the prostitutes even though they are really nice girls. Jaco is completely full of beautiful girls from all over the world. I enjoy the company of women and I would like to have a relationship but there is no way that I could ever be with some one that didn't know and understand my illness and willingly accept some of the extreme difficulties that my illness presents. There is only one girl I want to be with but she will have to be delivered from the lies of Christianity and leave the US to be with me. If this were to happen I might be encouraged to try again but short of being with Athea there is nothing in this world worth committing myself to and being sucked into an alternate reality or delusion when I know and understand that I am mentally ill. As long as I can survive in a reality where all I have to do is not kill myself, I win as long as I stay alive. If I forget that I am sick and I can't do the things I used to, then I am subject to mania and delusion. I know it will end in a crash and I will be more susceptible to suicide.

As long as I don't try then I can't fail and there is no reason to be depressed. There is no dishonor for me in this because no one could have tried harder to overcome a handicap than I have. If this handicap were physical, short of having my own pity party there would be nothing that could stop me from achieving my goals, But it's not; it is mental and I can not trust my own mind or emotions. To succeed you must believe and I realize that just because I see it or think it doesn't make it real and that there are a million alternate realities taking place with every thought in every mind in every second of every day. Any one of these realities can become truths to those who choose to believe in them and merely alternate perceptions of reality that I refuse to commit to, just thoughts or ideas no more.

I have a great deal of difficulty talking to my dad because at sixty nine years old he still has not come to grips with his or my schizophrenia and is constantly trying to suck me into his delusions. When I first wake up and say hello to him he instantly starts talking about money and business. We are both retired and we don't need to earn money but he just won't stop trying to make money. He spent what money we had left from the sale of our motel in Texas building me a business that I don't want and can't operate.

My dad just doesn't understand or believe that I'm mentally ill and that running a business is a total nightmare to me. I would much rather kill myself that be forced to live in a world of numbers always trying to destroy me. Taxes, payroll, inventory, rent, licenses, liabilities, advertising and bills, bills, bills.

He has been a very driven and successful person all his life and he just does not realize that I can't bring his visions to reality any more like I always had in the past. Before all he had to do was come up with an idea and fund it and I would do what it took to make it happen and we would share the profit.

Now even if I built a business I can't run it. When I deal with money figures I short out and that's all my dad lives for is to play the game of business. I didn't come back to Costa Rica to make a business this time I came here to hang out a while and try to enjoy life before I killed myself or completely lost what's left of my sanity. When I think about money I hate life and want to die.

Money has always been my enemy and no matter how much I made it was never enough. Now that I am mentally disabled and receive a pension I don't have to deal with the devaluation of my life through earnings as long as I live in a weaker economy than the US and can afford to live and care for myself.

Here in Costa Rica my rent and all of my bills combined are less than my electric bill was in Texas. I don't have much by standards in the States but to the Costa Ricans I am a Texas business man who is retired and still makes more than the average household earns. I am an artist and a musician and I am a master craftsman in many fields of construction but it is against the law for me to work, both as a term of my disability pension and my residency, so I don't.

I couldn't do it anyway, I just can't handle the stress any more. Just thinking about being involved in a large project causes me to become confused and scared. Not only of failure but that my next short circuit might be my last. After my last nervous/psychotic breakdown I realized that it was getting harder and harder to rebuild myself and that each time I returned the effects of the illness were worse. I have seen the leading edge of dementia and I understand how extreme the effects of schizophrenia can be. It has become my full time job to prevent myself from going there permanently or taking my own life just to end the struggle for sanity.

Caring for my dad and training my children Aaron and Natolie to cope with this disorder are my last obligations in life. I don't owe anyone anything. I have paid my debt to society, to God and to country. I was a faithful and loving husband but for now my wife has chosen Jesus over me. I was a patriot and a soldier but now the only cause worth fighting for is my own survival. I was a counselor, prophet and a priest for a God that didn't exist leading blind and foolish people astray in the name of hope. I never gave up trying until I realized that I had been disqualified from the game before I ever started. I never really had a chance to succeed or be normal, I had an abnormal brain in a world of normality.

CHAPTER TWENTY FOUR
LET'S TALK ABOUT MENTAL ILLNESS

The DSM-IV has become the bible for me now. It is as far as we know the truth. It is my salvation and the answer to life as I know it. If I study and indoctrinate myself in the scientific theories of neurological disorder then I truly arm myself against demonic attack and the forces of darkness. When knowledge and understanding are introduced superstition and ignorance fade into obscurity. When I was involved in Christianity I very seldom took the word of another pastor or teacher without researching the subject matter myself and developing my own theories before I reached a conclusion. Eating the watermelon and spitting out the seeds.

Un fortunately Christianity is based on circular reasoning so all of the opinions, commentary and alternate views were still all based on the same subject matter, the bible. As long as the bible is held as a standard of truth in your life and you hold the fundamental belief that it is inspired or holy, you commit yourself to a modified perception of reality where acceptance of delusional thinking is a requirement of faith. This certainly is not the prescription you would want to give someone that is subject to delusion.

If psychiatrist had the same motivation as pastors there would be a greater number of people that believed in mental health, but it's not a doctor's job to convince you of his diagnoses and his area of training is science and not salesmanship.

No one really wants to believe that they are mentally ill but everybody wants to believe that there is some other option, God.

When I cracked open my first book on Bi Polar disorder and started reading it I wept like the day that I found Jesus because I knew I had found the truth. It wasn't written in old English it hadn't been translated from ancient scrolls it wasn't holy or inspired by God. It was simply a book written by a doctor that explained to people what every MD practicing medicine in the field of mental health already knows. They might not know everything, but the data, symptoms and diagnostics available in that book were so self evident that after reading it I knew for an absolute fact that I was mentally ill and needed help and I wasn't going to get it from a church.

Hell I was the guy who counseled other people. As a clergy member I was a licensed counselor, I knew a great deal about human behavior. I was basically a mid evil psychologist practicing under a non sanctioned license. Most people don't know it, but pastors, priest and religious counselors are not required to hold any state license at all. They may have a license issued by a church or seminary but that license is only subject to the sect or denomination that they work for. In Texas there is no state licensing agency and there are no pre requisites what so ever. Even if they are degreed it is usually from a non affiliated Christian University that teaches religious doctrine instead of scientific theory. In fact I have often heard Pastor Walter Hallem publicly discourage the youth of his congregation from going to secular universities where they would be subject to the lies of this world. You know, lies like medicine and science.

You must always keep in mind that every licensed practitioner of medicine must be state board certified and have successfully completed a minimum of eight years of college plus internship. That's why religious counselors offer you free counseling and doctors charge you money. If a religious counselor can help you he gets 10% of your gross income instead of $100.00 per hour, not to mention brownie points in heaven.

Believing that I was not mentally ill in the name of Jesus wasn't going to make me well, but by believing that I was mentally ill sure answered a whole lot of questions that I had been trying to answer for decades. Why wasn't I normal and what the fuck was going on with my brain. It was almost embarrassing to think that everything that I had done for the past twenty years was because I was completely delusional. It was a leap of faith but I was completely sold on "juvenile onset, chronic, rapid cycling, Bi Polar 1 disorder", but I knew there was more.

I had been continually delusional and could easily experience mania and severe depression in a single day. I had been delusional for years at a time. The things that I read about normal Bi Polar symptoms made its victims look like sissies compared to the shit going on in my head but everything else was right on the money.

Let's keep in mind that I'm researching this in the wake of my last nervous or psychotic breakdown on my own, living in Art's Garage on a couch, isolated from all help because everyone I knew that could help me was a Christian. At this time I was pivoting on the edge of reality and then I got a book on schizophrenia.

After I read and understood the depths of psychosis and how severe the illness could become I was afraid. I understood that if I did not get a firm grip on reality that I was going to check out and not come back. I did not have the more severe symptoms of schizophrenia but I had a more consistent state of audio and visual hallucinations than present in Bi Polar disorder.

These symptoms were constant and accompanied mania, depression and good times too. Bi polar disorder normally cycles and these cycles can be monitored and mapped to some degree. My mania lasted until I crashed, I could live in a completely delusional based manic state of shamanistic euphoria for years at a time. When depression came and it did, I entered into a multi dimensional spiritual battle with Satan and his demonic forces until I defeated him through the power of Jesus.

I'm not shitting you at all, that's the way it was.

A lot of articles that I've read say that the term Schizoaffective Disorder is a catch all term that doctors use when they can't make an affirmative diagnoses. In my case I concluded the diagnoses myself before I ever saw a doctor. I knew that it was the only logical diagnoses for my condition. Well I wasn't a doctor, I was a researcher and a damn good one. I had just been researching the wrong curriculum for the answers. I had wasted fifteen years researching ancient fairy tales and religious commentary looking for the answers to everything.

When I took the next step and read a college level psychology book I understood everything. I didn't agree completely with everything but I damn sure knew a lot more than I did before. For instance; Freudian theorem and traditional psychiatry almost take as much faith as religion to believe, but the cognitive theory and neurosciences that have evolved from the early mental health sciences are no longer concepts and theories as much as they are accepted scientific fact. You see I'm not talking about sitting on a couch talking about your parents and trying to reach a hypothesis based on environment, experience, culture or upbringing. I'm talking about the fact that your brain has been genetically altered by some means and now your neurotransmitters are malfunctioning either too much or too little too fast or two slow. Dopamine, Serration, Glucosemines and their ability to flow through your synopsis.

It really is that simple and there's not a whole lot you can do about it. Every drug available for mental health disorders involving Bi polar and schizophrenia deal directly with these brain chemicals and their function. There's no great mystery here. The only question is how could this happen to me. Well although there are many camps on the subject of how, I think that other than coming to terms with yourself it is as irrelevant as wondering who made God or if chickens came before eggs. If you got it you need to deal with it and come to grips with reality. Let's take a look back any way just for shits and giggles.

1. I was born premature and had RH incompatibility syndrome. Research has shown links to the development of young adult schizophrenia in children born with this condition. Ok I'll buy that, I understand how that an undeveloped neuro-vascular system could affect the size of my synopsis and even the development of my responders.

2. Next I had a long history of crazy people on both sides of the family, My mom is depressive Bi Polar 2 and my dad is an absolutely amazing psychotic person, brilliantly twisted in a world according to himself but a great guy none the less. So I am a genetic candidate for both disorders if it's transferred through heredity.

OK I can buy that too, but wait there's more.

3. Remember the two brain concussions what about just plain old brain damage we can't rule out that.

So we've covered heredity, prenatal development and pre adolescent head trauma. If it were not for the fact that I personally know from my own understanding , experience and memory that I experienced hallucinations, out of body experiences and delusion as a small child I could not rule out the possibilities of drug induced psychosis.

4. Some researchers believe that Marijuana can induce schizophrenic affect and this is research and I can not rule out the possibility because I smoked Pot. You can go to .RxMarijuana.com and you will find a research study on the use of cannabis as a mood stabilizer in Bi Polar disorder. There is anecdotal evidence and a need for more clinical research.

My mom and dad didn't smoke and they were mentally ill and my sister didn't smoke and she was mentally ill. Everyone else that I knew that smoked it wasn't necessarily mentally ill so I wrote it off as more anti marijuana bullshit. The effects of mind altering drugs on normal people are much different than those of a person with an altered mind.

I have never experienced the affects of marijuana described in the DSM-IV or other medical journals. For me the effect of marijuana stops the psychosis. The lulling or stoned affect experienced by a normal person is just enough to stop the voices so I only hear a single thought process. Kind of like a Spam blocker on the Internet. Pot has the ability to bring me out of a depressive suicidal episode in minutes instead of days. When normal people smoke pot they can become unmotivated. I suffer from delusions of grandeur and run the risk of psychosis and mania, marijuana stabilizes my thoughts and allows me to reason and prevents mania and anxiety. When I moved to Costa Rica I learned for the first time that Marijuana doesn't cause paranoia, getting busted in the States does.

In Texas if you or anyone in your household have ever been busted for pot, any amount, at any time in your life, you are completely ineligible for any state assistance including food stamps, prescriptions or psychiatric care from the HMMR, but you can get benefits if you are an illegal alien. Go figure that, sorry Charley no help for you Pot Heads !

Remember neuro science? While high doses of Delta 9THC of up to 50% found in today's hybrid hydroponics have been found to cause temporary psychotic affect in schizophrenia patients, regular sativa with lower levels of THC contain other canibinoids like CB1 and CB2 that manipulate canibanoid receptors in the cerebral cortex that effect Bi polar disorder by blocking serotonin receptors .

Wow, how about that.

So is marijuana the cause or the cure ?

I say marijuana keeps me from killing myself and is a whole lot better than the $ 1000 dollar a month prescription cocktail I was taking in the states that almost killed me. Zanex withdrawal was one of the worst experiences of psychosis in my life. Thanks Doc.

But I had much bigger fish to fry.

Numbers 5. 6. And 7.

From the time that I was thirteen until my Christian salvation at twenty I had done enough

5. LSD (acid),

6. MDMA (ecstasy) and

7. Psilocybin (mushrooms)

to have flown to the moon and back a couple of times, in fact I think I might have.

The point is that if all the other prevailing factors weren't in place I was still a candidate for HPPD or Hallucinogen Persisting Perception Disorder.

Guess what, this disorder has the same exact symptoms and treatment as, You guessed it; Schizoaffective disorder 295.7.

Do you get the point yet I had seven different valid possibilities of why I had the disorder and all I had to do was accept the fact that I had it, not figure out how.

I do know that if you have an HPPD diagnoses you don't get a government pension or disability benefits and if you have Bi Polar or Schizophrenia you do, so don't blame the acid if you want to get help. Besides the results and the treatments are the same regardless of what causes the illness the only difference might be in the therapy stage if you have issues to deal with in understanding and acceptance. It's a heavy trip to think that you're mentally scared for life because you partied to hard as a teenager but you can't rule out the possibility.

I personally believe that since the psychedelic drugs affect the 5 HT responders in the cerebral cortex that mimic the effects of these type of mental disorders it is obvious that when in later life someone experiences similar effects without the presence of the outside stimuli, they naturally assume that they are experiencing a relapse of their past drug induced experiences. For a person who has experienced the affect of mind altering drugs it would be easy to correlate the similarities between a psychedelic trip and the effects of psychosis. In fact how better could you explain a hallucination than to compare an acid trip.

Well I never had a bad trip and I never had a negative experience on mind altering drugs, but I had been running from ghost and demons since I was a child. It was depression and mania that led me to drugs in the first place.

I had a pre disposition for co morbidity long before I fucked up my brain on drugs and alcohol if the heredity guys were right and besides there is still a couple of million people who never did drugs and have schizophrenia and millions of people that have taken mind altering drugs that don't. Just like researching the bible you can't conclude a theory without substantial supportive evidence and unless every person that ever tripped on acid developed HPPD there is no conclusive evidence to show that this rare group of individuals who are diagnosed with HPPD were not already predisposed candidates for schizophrenia or Bi Polar in the first place and a doctor can not tell the difference. You just get labeled as a burn out and you don't get a pension check because you were misdiagnosed.

Ok so you're mentally ill what now?

Understanding and knowledge have been the only help that I have had since being diagnosed and leaving the United States. Educating myself about my illness along with marijuana treatment and living on the beach are what I have done to save myself from myself. I have never spent a day in counseling because, once you've read the counselors instruction manual it's kind of like exposing the Wizard of OZ and seeing behind the curtain. I had already dealt with all my psychological issues through Christianity. You know forgiving your father and loving yourself and all that bullshit. I taught that crap to other people for years, I was already completely past all that way before I had ever seen a psychiatrist. I am really thankful that Dr Kathy at my MHMR realized that and never patronized me. He respected the fact that I had diagnosed myself and done my research and immediately classified me as a level three patient and didn't recommend therapy. I mean sure it's great to get things off your chest but at $100 bucks an hour you can go smoke a joint and write it down in a journal or write a book, it's good therapy.

Instead of just listening unfortunately most counselors and therapist want to help you, so after you finish whining they give you advice. Lots of it is good advice, but any one that is from a Judeo/Christian background whether a licensed practitioner or a clergy member is going to give you advice and recommendations based on religious theology that will only perpetuate your delusions and keep you in a state of psychosis.

Therapist that encourage their patients to get involved in faith or religion are simply passing off their patients to a world of delusion where they can function in a robot society of fairy tales instead of healing them with truth and reality. Not to mention the tremendous liability involved in prescribing a treatment of un safe and unhealthy religious involvement that promote trains of thought that induce prejudice, fear, psychotic behavior and much worse.

Remember hypnotism is not a cure for mental illness and hypnotizing yourself to believe that Jesus healed you is not going to do anything for your but extend your period of psychosis and make it more difficult for you to keep a firm grip on reality. If you feel like you need to be forgiven, for God's sake forgive yourself, after all sin is established by religion in the first place and creates a ubiquitous cycle of acceptance and denial.

You haven't fallen short of anything except a lot of stupid prerequisites established by a religious society and the expectations of others that do not understand that you are mentally ill and therefore separate and different than the cultural norms of society. Now that's not a license to shit on everyone but you must understand that you will never be like all the other kids. You're different and unique. You are one percent of the world's population and can not ever be expected to fit into the norms of any society without being subject to delusion. The societal standards set forth as normality for everyone else, is a living hell for me and an unrealistic goal that I can never achieve. It's not my fault it's just the way it is.

I am mentally ill. On the other side of the coin you are herded along into the other category where you are segregated from society with the severely handicapped, the mentally retarded and the insane because you have a mental disability. Mania and delusion can be contagious when you get around other mentally ill people and a mental institution is not the healthiest place in the world to be. Helping other people can be very therapeutic and rewarding for some but for now I can only help myself and my children. I hated sitting around the MHMR waiting to be seen with all the other crazy people. I wanted to talk to my doctor, get my meds, talk to the kid's doctors and counsel with them and then get the hell out of there.

CHAPTER TWENTY FIVE
CHARASMANIA
PHYCHOSIS AND RELIGION

I realize the need for a more comprehensive study of some of the theories and experiences discussed in the book. This was as I intended it to be, my story and nothing else. I felt no need to go into great detail about the doctrines and scriptures referenced in the book because I didn't want to lose the interest of the non doctrine savvy readers and still get my point across. I realize to many of you both agnostic and Religious alike you are searching for absolute truths and definitive answers and need to know everything there is to know about something and I admire that.

The Bible teaches us to study that we may show ourselves approved, a workman that doesn't need to be ashamed and it's right in that respect. We only need to stand in shame when we let ourselves remain in the vast expanse of ignorance necessary to sustain an unrealistic delusional existence perpetuated by the ancient ramblings of madmen written down two thousand years ago.

I will not attempt to prove whether Jesus was God's son, or resurrected or validate the stories of the bible because honestly those points are aimless and non productive. I have spent years arguing Christian apologetics and defending the Christian faith and what I'm attempting to reveal is far beyond the envelope of arguing doctrine with religious fanatics.

For example; We all go see " Star Wars" together, afterwards we all go to the coffee shop and you guys are discussing maters within the context of the film (The Bible GET IT!) and we are discussing George Lucas (Realizing of course that it was only a story, written by a man).

I think it's a good example and an explanation of why this book is far beyond proving or disproving the Bible, but will attempt to show clearly that if you believe the Bible with all of your heart and practice it's doctrines and apply it's theories to your life you will ultimately commit yourself to a life of psychosis and delusion.

The other day I was pondering a phrase as I so often do as I remembered the words of Mr. Fred Rogers from Mr. Rogers Neighborhood on PBS (a Presbyterian minister I might add).

Mr. Rogers always said "Welcome to the world of make believe" when his show came on. The World of make believe or to make the world believers, to make believers of the world or as Mark 16 said "Go Ye into all the world making believers". I know that this is just a funny play on words but the point is, unless you are indoctrinated as a child or someone takes advantage of you during a period of duress it takes a professional evangelist (a trained sales person) and the peer pressure of other believers such as friends and family to make you accept the Bible as anything more than just a compilation of old stories and fables. In fact; I can think of no other book that anyone could ever hand you that would hold the weight of eternal damnation or nirvana upon your acceptance of it's content. Well not necessarily, I was handed a psychology book and told that if I didn't accept what it had to say I would in fact be committed to a life of Hell and agony on earth, as long as I continued to believe the Bible and fuel my delusions with the spiritual subject matter held within the context of Bible Based Christian doctrine.

You see I came to a point in my life where I had to stand in a place beyond the realm of merely believing. I was forced to make a choice between choosing to believe the Bible or my interpretation thereof and living in an unreal parallel dimension where I spoke to God ,Angels and Demons and was tormented by Satan or accept the fact that none of these things were real and what I was experiencing was in fact psychosis fueled by my beliefs in Christianity and perpetuated by religious practice. Now I'm not saying that Christianity is the cause for my schizophrenia or anyone else's, What I am saying is that the modern day church is nothing more than a free outpatient clinic for the mentally ill (free except for 10% of your income) and that professing to believe in the bible actually qualifies you to be mentally ill by today's modern diagnostic standards.

Although in the past unfortunately, choosing to believe in the bible meant social acceptance, eternal fire insurance and a ticket to heaven as well as the very popular belief that you would be tried and killed for witchcraft because you were an unbeliever and not a member of the local church. That was always a popular motivating force.

In today's more modern world people are finally more inclined to choose to be labeled sane as there is a much greater stigma about being mentally ill than there is about going to hell. I had to choose the former of the two. I could no longer exist in a world where the Bible was true and protect my state of mental well being.

Either the Bible was a lie and there aren't parallel dimensions of metaphysical beings warring for our souls or I was condemned to a life of torment and anguish fighting a never ending battle with Satan and his forces defending righteousness and the cross of Jesus for an ultimate reward in the afterlife. The answer was clear to me, I had already spent fifteen years fighting demons and listening to God's voice and when I made a decision to step out in true faith and denounce Christianity just to see for myself what the truth really was. This is not to be taken lightly. To take such a stand in the search for ultimate truth in itself is a messianic quality. I basically committed spiritual suicide forfeiting the grandeur of heaven and even eventually destroying my marriage and career to see once and for all what the definitive truth of this matter was.

In my case I found out that I was mentally ill and needed help. In your case hopefully you will just discover that you're wasting your life and spending all of your time and money throwing it all away on ancient myths, legends and folklore. If Christianity was a club and we all just tried to do good things like Jesus, it would be cool but it's not. Christianity by definition is a sectarian religious cult movement just like all the other religions and as a term of faith you are requested to believe that the Bible is in fact the inspired word of God which in turn leads to a profession of belief in absolutely impossible concepts of metaphysics that unknowingly traps us in a world of unrealism and delusion.

The study of secular theology and psychiatry where taboo in the church. Just as early Catholicism taught that the holy scripture could only be interpreted by the priest who led to the Protestant reformation, modern day theorist can only substantiate their claims of absolute truth by forbidding the study of secular reasoning, science and psychology. When knowledge and education are applied to myths and fables, truths are analyzed under a different spectrum of light casting shadows on archaic theories once taught as absolute truths. It was only when I removed myself from a Judeo Christian society and culture that I realized that what I held as absolute truths were merely the embodiment of my own personal beliefs and a reflection of the programming that I had received from a group of irrational individuals that's sole purpose for existence is for all the world to join them in their quest for universal dominion and oneness with spirituality (taking over the world in Jesus Name). "That every knee shall bow and every tongue shall confess on both heaven and earth that Jesus Christ is Lord to the glory of the father".

In the words of the modern day philosophers Cheech and Chong "Wow that's some heavy shit man!".

To push the rational brain beyond reason is the essence of spiritual belief, but to engage in un healthy psychotic behavior that stands outside of rational thought such as forcing oneself to believe concepts far beyond ones personal scope of reference and filling in the blanks with faith does not constitute a true personal belief but more of the existential leap of faith. If you were to say, wait and let me go to college and study history and psychology before I conform myself to such an unrealistic belief system, you would need to be discouraged from illuminating yourself in the ways of the world and the lies of Satan, because those books are secular and products of the mind of man which is the tool of Satan at enmity with God. No one would ever invite you to openly discuss the possibility that anything in the Bible was not true because it would destroy the very foundations of Christian faith.

CHAPTER TWENTYSIX
BEFORE WE REALY SAY GOODBYE

Before we say goodbye I would briefly like to touch on a few personal points that were discussed in the previous chapters. Although I come off as being pissed off some time (and rightly so) I'm not . I'm not a Christian Basher, in fact I will be the first to tell you that some of the finest people that I have ever met have been Believers. I spent fifteen years of my life ministering to the needs of others and leading untold thousands to the knowledge of Christ through personal witness, preaching, street ministry and music ministry and yes Demonic Deliverance Ministry too.

Before I indoctrinated myself in basic Christian dogma, I had no moral guidelines or standards in my life and without the application of religious legalism enforced by eternal damnation I did not possess the personal will power necessary to keep myself from sin. But you know what, the Army was capable of achieving the same thing in just eight weeks of training but unfortunately both organizations request the sacrifice of your life as payment for this fine training. The gentlemen that wrote the books that I had read on Psychology paid for four years of university training in general applications before paying for post graduate and doctrinal studies equaling about ten years of college plus internship before they started spouting out their bias opinionated theories. So we can gather that the lessons of self preservation must come at a really high price.

Who of the three afore mentioned would have the purest motive ? The motive of the Christian can never be truly pure. Christianity needs You to validate it's self because the greatest ruling factor in its favor is popular consensus. The beliefs of the Christian can only be validated on earth if you choose to believe them too. Their very plight against the odds of reality hinges on your acceptance of their belief, as a matter of fact it is so important that you will be condemned to Hell for not agreeing with them.

That's pretty serious! And just like it's the mandate of Islamic extremist to kill for jihad it is the Christian's mandate to convert or condemn all of mankind and this is his purpose for existence.

Next the Drill Sergeant. His motive is pure but certainly not in your favor. Oh he's your buddy and he'll take care of you but always remember that his primary objective is to develop a winning team of highly motivated killers. He can offer you a world of certain unarguable realism like his boot in your ass or you will die if you don't follow orders. OK here we go with absolutism again. Wasn't it the great philosophers DEVO that taught us that freedom from choice is what we really want?

As long as I am free from personal choice or decision I seem to excel. I wonder why that is? " NOT".

How many of you ever excelled in sports after your coach stopped yelling at you?

OK now the Psychoanalyst. If this guy misdiagnoses you it could destroy his career and potentially lead to a patients attempted suicide or death. Although he charges you a lot of money " Almost as much as a prostitute" he is forced to charge a lot to cover the cost of the mal practice insurance necessary to protect him against you when he tells you that you need help and you tell him that he's crazy.

Not only did I not have the motivation to put myself through ten tears of higher education, if I did, it sure as hell wouldn't be so I could sit around and talk to crazy people. Oh these guys are out to get your money " get for real " I only listened to other people's problems because the voices in my head told me to, I would have never done it for any amount of money. I hated being forced to have compassion on people that I thought were dumb asses. Remember I'm BI Polar. Explaining obvious problems to people with their head up their ass is not at all fun. Not to mention the real therapy that goes on with truly mentally ill people that are given a much better quality of life when under the care of a loving professional.

Now I'm out here on my own for the first time in 39 years. No wife, no Jesus, no God, no Drill Sergeant and not even a psychiatrist. They have all done their part and I have graduated everyone's course with flying colors. My wall is covered with pretty pieces of paper that say what a smart and great guy I am and list my many accomplishments. But just as eternal reward comes after this life is over. My illumination and understanding of life as I know it only came to me after the realization that I was Permanently mentally impaired and my perceptions of reality were distorted and not to be trusted. It also cost me the highest price to realize and believe this. Not only did I divorce my Christian wife who I love dearly, I had to leave the church, default heaven and be labeled as permanently mentally disabled to be in this popular club of unbelievers with no hope. But yet there is still hope for us.

Well in closing I would like to say good luck, if reading my story has benefited anyone in any way it almost makes it all worthwhile. Please don't take my word for the information that I've presented, research for yourselves and make your own determinations. Both the internet and the local library have a wealth of information available that can help you make the transition from an ignorant victim wandering in the dark to a proactive participant in your own recovery.

If you are a mental health professional, thanks. I hope that reading my experiences might offer you an alternate viewpoint or give you a different perspective in helping treat your patients. I know it has sure helped me.

If I could believe in anything I would choose to believe that my wife Athea might someday read this story and put down her cross, sacrifice the false reality of heaven and hell, denounce Christianity and come live with me in paradise. This like any other delusion is, and can only exist as a dream until reality is applied and action has occurred. Like so many others Athea's been brain washed for so long that Christianity has become her identity and she can no longer think for herself she can only quote bible scriptures and respond to the voices in her head that she believes are spirits.

Thank You.

The Rev Nathon Q. Dees
AKA Jaco Nate, Guru AkhNathon
Or Texas Guitar Legend Nathon Dees
NathonsPlace@aol.com

www.ingramcontent.com/pod-product-compliance
Lightning Source LLC
Chambersburg PA
CBHW070355310526
45790CB00017B/773